How to survive in the jungle of

Enterprise Architecture Frameworks

Creating or choosing an

Enterprise Architecture Framework

To learn more about the described topics, its author, speaking engagements, or research requests, visit the official homepage of the Institute For Enterprise Architecture Developments at http://www.enterprise-architecture.info.

Cover Art, layout and editorial writing by Jaap Schekkerman.

Printed in Victoria, Canada

Note for Librarians: a cataloguing record for this book that includes Dewey Classification and US Library of Congress numbers is available from the National Library of Canada. The complete cataloguing record can be obtained from the National Library's online database at:
www.nlc-bnc.ca/amicus/index-e.html
ISBN 1-4120-1607-x

TRAFFORD

This book was published on-demand in cooperation with Trafford Publishing.
On-demand publishing is a unique process and service of making a book available for retail sale to the public taking advantage of on-demand manufacturing and Internet marketing. On-demand publishing includes promotions, retail sales, manufacturing, order fulfilment, accounting and collecting royalties on behalf of the author.

Suite 6E, 2333 Government St., Victoria, B.C. V8T 4P4, CANADA
Phone 250-383-6864   Toll-free 1-888-232-4444 (Canada & US)
Fax 250-383-6804   E-mail sales@trafford.com   Web site www.trafford.com
TRAFFORD PUBLISHING IS A DIVISION OF TRAFFORD HOLDINGS LTD.
Trafford Catalogue #03-1984   www.trafford.com/robots/03-1984.html

10   9   8   7   6   5   4

How to survive in the jungle of

Enterprise Architecture Frameworks

Creating or choosing an

Enterprise Architecture Framework

Jaap Schekkerman

Second Edition

2004

The Institute For Enterprise Architecture Developments intended not to use any copyrighted material for this publication or, if not possible, to indicate the copyright or source of the respective object. All TradeMarks, ServiceMarks and registered trademarks / servicemarks mentioned in this publication are the property of their respective organisations. The copyright for any material created by the author is reserved.

Second Edition

This second edition is an update of the first edition published December 2003 with some refinements and enhancements on several pages and a refreshment and actual update of the tools selection paragraph, due to changes in the Enterprise Architecture tooling market.

Cover Art, layout and editorial writing by Jaap Schekkerman.

First Edition 2003.

Research for this Book

Research for this book is done by the Institute For Enterprise Architecture Developments *[IFEAD]*. Several public domain documents and information sources are discovered, analysed and revised. References to these sources are added in this book in several ways; however the access to these sources over time is out of the scope of IFEAD. The information provided is of a general nature only, which is not intended to address the specific circumstances of any particular individual or organisation; not necessarily comprehensive, complete, accurate or up to date.

Purpose of this Book

Several times in my Enterprise Architecture (EA) practice, people asked me which framework shall I adopt or what are the benefits of the Zachman framework over TOGAF, etc. Others asked me to help them to define their own corporate EA framework. Before answering these types of questions, it is important to know what the differences and commonalities are of these frameworks and standards.

This book explains the role of Enterprise Architecture Frameworks and shows the differences between the most popular Enterprise Architecture Frameworks now a day available in the world.

With the growing importance of Enterprise Architecture [EA]* at the same time, the discussion started how to create or choose the right Enterprise Architecture Framework & Tools for your organisation in the jungle of the existing ones.

Giving an overview of the history of most Enterprise Architecture frameworks as well as their purpose, scope, principles, structure, guidance and compliance, will support you in identifying the usefulness of these Enterprise Architecture frameworks for your own situation. For the in-depth details of the described Enterprise Architecture Frameworks, references to the original sources of information are added in the chapter References & Bibliography.

Separate chapters are addressing the most popular Enterprise Architecture tools on the market and their support of existing frameworks.

---

* *For most text in brackets, a clarification or reference of the acronym can be found in the glossary and reference chapters.*

Audience

This book is composed to serve Enterprise Architects, (IT) Managers, and Program managers, CEO's, CIO's, System or Solution Architects, Students and all others interested in Enterprise Architecture Frameworks and approaches.

Content

1 What is Enterprise Architecture about?

1.1 Introduction

This chapter discusses Enterprise Architectures as they relate to the broad decisions that must be made by organisations to compete or survive in an ever-changing world. The concept of Enterprise Architecture has been defined and discussed variously in extant articles and in practitioner and research publications for the last years. Let us take a look to a holistic view of diverse interpretations.

1.2 The holistic view

Enterprise Architecture is a complete expression of the enterprise; a master plan which *"acts as a collaboration force"* between aspects of business planning such as goals, visions, strategies and governance principles; aspects of business operations such as business terms, organisation structures, processes and data; aspects of automation such as information systems and databases; and the enabling technological infrastructure of the business such as computers, operating systems and networks.

In a large modern enterprise, a rigorously defined framework is necessary to be able to capture a vision of the *"entire*

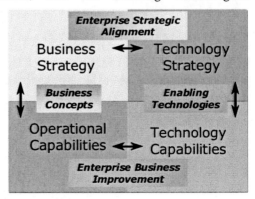

organisation" in all its dimensions and complexity. Enterprise Architecture (EA) is a program supported by frameworks, which is able to coordinate the many facets that make up the fundamental essence of an enterprise at a holistic way.

1.3   Enterprise Architecture Program

Enterprise Architecture provides a mechanism that enables communication about the essential elements and functioning of the enterprise.

It yields centralized, stable, and consistent information about the enterprise environment. In an insurance company, for example, an EA would help executives pinpoint the companies more lucrative markets, understand how well the company's current resources are meeting customer needs in those locations, and determine what kind of systems might be needed to improve services.

The precise, high-quality information an EA provides also makes it much easier for the organisation to respond to the forces of change and make better decisions. And finally, because an EA enables organisations to reduce duplication and inconsistencies in information, they can dramatically improve ROI for future IT implementations common architecture information and building a repository to store it.

Focusing on Enterprise Architecture is focusing added value to the business in terms of ROI [Return on Information] and at the same time streamlining the technology to reduce complexity and costs.

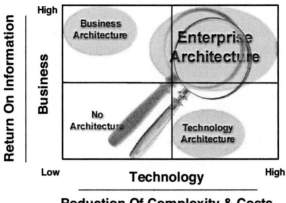

Reduction Of Complexity & Costs

This EA program addresses at a holistic way the elements of strategy, frameworks, the overall EA process, methods & techniques, standards and tools. In this book, the focus is on EA frameworks and the area of popular EA tools.

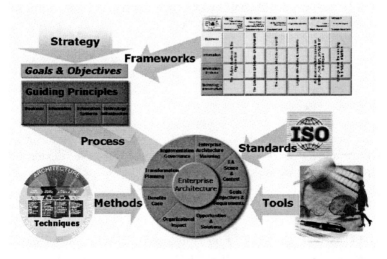

EA Program and its elements

1.3.1   Analogy

"There is a parallel between Enterprise Architecture design and city planning. City planners must design in the face of many unknowns, such as future transportation technologies, changing work, living, and commuting patterns, and so on." "As a result of this level of planning, our major cities are able to accommodate new technologies for transportation and communication which remain viable for hundreds of years, and which make a major contribution to each city's brand of urban culture." [Nolan and Mulryan, 1987]

1.4   Fundamental Enterprise Architecture Principles

- Always design a thing by considering it in its overall context

A fundamental principle that can be applied to Enterprise Architecture is: "Always design a thing by considering it in its next larger context - a chair in a room, a room in a house, a house in an environment, an environment in a city plan." *[Saarinen, 1956]*

Enterprise Architecture maps the design of the larger context (i.e. the enterprise) within which organisational design, business process reengineering, systems design, technology infrastructure design and data analysis, should be considered. Also, the Enterprise Architecture is part of the Extended Enterprise environment and should also consider the external environmental variables.

- Not to foresee, but to enable

The French aviator and writer Antoine de Saint-Exupery *[Saint-Exupery]* in one of his novels wrote:
"As for the future, your task is not to foresee, but to enable it".

In Enterprise Architecture as in city planning it is futile to attempt to foresee every possible future change. The enterprise architecture must rather provide the capability to enable change to occur rapidly, without undue resource utilisation, yet in a controlled manner and with minimal adverse impact.

- Strategic Vision is Leading

Professor William R. King *[King, 1995]* suggests that the guiding enterprise architecture of organisations should be based on the strategic vision. In other words, this vision bridges the extant status of the firm ("Where it is?") and its projected future status ("Where it wants to be?").

The strategic vision is related to the firm's current and future capabilities. The guiding dictum is that: a single capability of the firm cannot provide a sustainable competitive advantage to the firm. The firm cannot compete on the basis of 'low cost' or 'best quality' or 'customer service.'

The sustainable competitive advantage of the firm derives from the "synergy" of the firm's various capabilities. Porter *[Porter]* has proposed a similar concept in his notion of "complementarities." He argues that the various competitive capabilities of the firm should be "complementary" or "synergistic" so that the synergy resulting from them cannot be easily imitated by current or potential competitors.

It is worth considering that the same argument has been made with reference to different business - technology related innovations, such as the more recent communication technology possibilities (Internet, wireless, etc.) and the discussions about the benefits of Enterprise Architecture.

- The Only Constant is Dynamics

Dynamics is the only constant while adaptiveness is the natural variable. *[Schekkerman]*

- Good is Good Enough

An Enterprise Architect knows he has achieved the perfect solution not when there is nothing left to add, but when there is, nothing left to take away. *[Saint-Exupery]*

- Spirit & Creativity

Pure logic is the ruin of the spirit and creativity delivers unexpected opportunities. *[Saint-Exupery]*

- Teaching Enterprise Architects

If you want to create an Enterprise Architecture, don't drum up the architects to collect information and don't assign them tasks and work, but rather teach them to long for the endless value creating possibilities of the enterprise. *[Saint-Exupery]*

2 Enterprise Architecture in Context

Recent Surveys of CEO's, CIO's and other executives provide some evidence of the growing importance of Enterprise Architecture over the last few years. In one of the most recent studies of the Institute For Enterprise Architecture Developments[1], Enterprise Architecture was ranked near the top of the list of most important issues considered by CEO's and CIO's.

Apparently, this suggests the significance of the overarching framework within which the various aspects of decision-making and development are considered: including Business Architecture, Information Architecture, Information-Systems Architecture (Data Architecture), Technology Infrastructure Architecture and things like Software Architecture.

The various decisions related to business development and technology innovations need to be considered in a systemic manner within the framework of various architectures. Choices of methods and techniques have to be made in the context of the goals and objectives.

So, what is the problem? Many organisations have been paralysed by the complexity of the business & technology and the rate of change in business & technology. Organisations that have decided to pursue IT projects still show an unacceptably high failure rate: *IT project failures in industry and Government account for an astounding $75 billion in losses each year, according to Gartner Inc*[2].

---

[1]*Institute For Enterprise Architecture Developments, EA Survey 2003; http://www.enterprise-architecture.info*
[2] *Gartner Inc.; http://www3.gartner.com/Init*

Our great leap forward in business & technology driven productivity has created a plethora of overlapping and confusing solutions, products and standards that increase the complexity and risks associated with every decision a CEO and CIO makes.

Exaggerated claims by vendors and standards bodies promoting the latest panacea product or standard are mind numbing. It is extremely difficult to construct an Enterprise Architecture based framework that properly relates the vast array of overlapping solutions, products and standards, much less an enterprise framework that can be explained to financial decision-makers or the end user community.

All this puts Business & IT executives at a crossroads. There are tremendous rewards for organisations that are able to harness the vast array of available options into a holistic EA framework of flexible domains and supportive technology that meet the rapidly evolving needs of their stakeholder communities. Enterprise Architecture process and framework must effectively align business & IT resources and processes that they enable.

Developing a system based on the EA results is asking modelling methods that comply with the system development environment. Supporting decision-making is asking other type of modelling methods and techniques.

So, besides the choices for an EA framework at the same time choices for supporting methods and techniques has to be made.

The decisions related to strategy, business goals, information needs, data mapping, selection of product- independent systems, and selection of specific hardware and software need to be guided by this framework to ensure maximal effectiveness and efficiency.

Unfortunately, while most Enterprise Architecture frameworks and processes that are gaining currency are able to generate good descriptive architecture models, they do not create actionable, extended enterprise architectures that address today's rapidly evolving complex collaborative environments.

2.1 Enterprise Architecture definitions

The world has not really settled on precise definitions of architecture or architecture description as these terms relate to enterprises, systems, or software. The Institute of Electrical and Electronics Engineers *[IEEE]* (see ANSI/IEEE 1471-2000[3]), the US Department of Defence *[DoD]*, and various business and technology authorities do, however, generally agree that architecture is about the structure of important things (systems or enterprises), their components, and how the components fit and work together to fulfil some purpose.

- Some well known Enterprise Architecture Definitions

'Enterprise Architecture is about understanding all of the different elements that go to make up the enterprise and how those elements inter-relate'

The Open Group

"Enterprise Architecture is a strategic information asset base, which defines the business mission, the information necessary to perform the mission, the technologies necessary to perform the mission, and the transitional processes for implementing new technologies in response to the changing mission needs."

USA Federal CIO Council

---

[3] *ANSI/IEEE 1471-2000; http://www.ieee.org/portal/index.jsp*

"Enterprise Architecture is the holistic expression of an organisation's key business, information, application and technology strategies and their impact on business functions and processes. The approach looks at business processes, the structure of the organisation, and what type of technology is used to conduct these business processes."

Meta Group, Inc.

2.1.1   Key Definitions in this context

Architecture
The structure of elements, their interrelationships and the principles and guidelines governing their design and evolution over time.

Elements
A good definition of "elements" in this context are all the elements that enclose the areas of People, Processes, Business and Technology. In that sense, examples of elements are: strategies, business drivers, principles, stakeholders, units, locations, budgets, domains, functions, processes, services, information, communications, applications, systems, infrastructure, etc.

Enterprise
A good definition of "enterprise" in this context is any collection of organisations that has a common set of goals/principles and/or single bottom line. In that sense, an enterprise can be a whole corporation, a division of a corporation, a government organisation, a single department, or a network of geographically distant organisations linked together by common objectives.

Baseline or As-Is Enterprise Architecture
The set of products that portray the existing enterprise, the current business practices, and IT infrastructure. Commonly referred to as the As-Is Enterprise Architecture.

Target or To-Be Enterprise Architecture

The set of products that portray the future or end-state enterprise, generally captured in the organisation's strategic thinking and business & technology plans. Commonly referred to as the To-Be Enterprise Architecture.

Transformation or sequencing Plan

A document that defines the strategy for changing the enterprise from the current baseline to the target enterprise architecture. It schedules multiple, concurrent, interdependent activities, and incremental builds that will evolve the enterprise.

Enterprise Architecture products or results

The visualisations, graphics, models, and/or narrative that depicts the enterprise environment and design.

2.2 Type of Architectures

An Enterprise Architecture relates organisational mission, goals, and objectives to business tasks, activities and relations and to the technology or IT infrastructure required to execute them.

A System or Solution Architecture relates requirements and the external world to system / solution structures, including both hardware and software, so that the effectiveness of a system design concept can be communicated.

A Software Architecture relates requirements, fixed system hardware, and infrastructure (i.e., COTS or GOTS) to software structures in order to demonstrate software effectiveness.

Other views of architecture, such as governance and security are emerging.

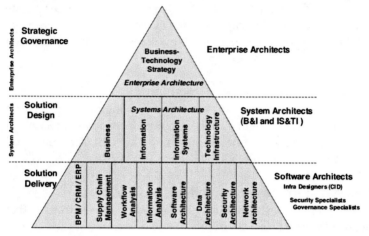

There are common aspects among all these architecture types. They are models that convey structures as the fulfilment of some purpose or need, and they facilitate reasoning and communication about properties of the entities modelled.

3 Critical Success Factors for Enterprise Architectures

An effective Enterprise Architecture approach and accompanying framework and methodology produces Enterprise Architectures that:

- o Create and maintain a common vision of the future shared by both the business and IT, driving continuous business/IT alignment
- o Create a holistic, end-to-end future-state enterprise architecture process that accurately reflects the business strategy of the enterprise
- o Build agility by lowering the "complexity barrier," an inhibitor of change
- o Increase the flexibility of the enterprise in linking with external partners
- o Develop a proactive organisation capable of meeting customer demands, outpacing the competition, and driving innovation
- o Reduce risk and prepare the enterprise for rapid, unplanned change
- o Avoid the pitfalls of business-unit IT functions operating at odds with one another
- o Institute a program of progressive technology refinement
- o Create, unify, and integrate business processes across the enterprise
- o Unlock the power of information, unifying information silos that hinder corporate initiatives such as customer relationship management and e-business
- o Eliminate duplicate and overlapping technologies, decreasing support costs

o Reduce solution delivery time and development costs by maximizing reuse of technology, information, and business applications

To accomplish this, an Enterprise Architecture approach must be:

Holistic in Scope: It must address all aspects of the Extended Enterprise and directly associated with business technology alignment: business structure, business activities, business processes, information flows, information-systems, and infrastructure, standards, policies. The notion of "Extended Enterprising" is growing in importance, and extends stakeholder status to include external value net members. Most enterprise architecture efforts are too inwardly focused, and do not include the customers and key business partners. This results in miss-aligned enterprise architectures, and lost opportunities to gain competitive advantage and government effectiveness. The "Extended Enterprising" focus directly supports Business 2 Business initiatives, E-Government and cross- community initiatives critical to global trading and communication today.

Collaboration Based: The effort must include representatives from all key stakeholders and value net members into the EA program: business domains, senior management, business partners, and customers. This is critical to obtaining "buy-in," ongoing support and business / partner, customer alignment and collaboration.

Alignment Driven: It must address the need to directly align 'extended' business and technology drivers in a way that is comprehensible and transparent to all key stakeholders, with a continued process of tracing enterprise architecture initiatives to the business strategy.

Value Driven: It must provide mechanisms to define business cases that help ensure and demonstrate the business value of enterprise architecture solutions.

Dynamic Environments: It must include analytical methods that support the development of enterprise architectures that are flexible and dynamic to changing business drivers, new opportunities or roadblocks, and enterprise architectures that provide transformation options that mitigate risks and are flexible and dynamic to budget and other organisational constraints.

Normative Results: It must provide the ability to define solution sets that can be measured, validated and mapped to real world solutions.

Non-Prescriptive: It must not presume an implementation approach. That is out of the scope of the enterprise architecture program.

4 Key Concepts of holistic Enterprise Architectures

An overall holistic Enterprise Architecture includes all the elements presented in the Extended Enterprise Architecture (E2A) Framework below.

While this framework is important, in that it outlines all the enterprise architectural artefacts required, it does not completely address the actionable aspects of an enterprise architecture, which deal with business technology alignment, validation and actual integration into the organisation.

These must be supported with an effective combined approach for enterprise program management and enterprise architecture to implement.

E2AF	Why? Vision / Strategy Business / Technology Drivers Scope Contextual Level	With Who? Value Net Relations Cooperating / Collaborating Elements Environmental Level	What? Goals & Objectives Requirements Conceptual Level	How? Logical Representation Logical Level	With what? Solution Representation Physical Level	When? Enterprise Impact Transformational Level
Business						
Information	The Future Business & the Organisation	The Extended Enterprise Environment	The concepts, what do we want?	Logical directions & solutions	Physical solutions based on change, redesign, products or techniques	Change from the existing to a future situation
Information– Systems						
Technology – Infrastructure						

Extended Enterprise Architecture (E2A) Framework

The Extended Enterprise Architecture (E2A) Framework is developed to meet existing and future evolving complex enterprise collaboration environments.

4.1 Focusing on Alignment, Validation and Ability to Implement

Developing a complete enterprise architectural model of every element in the organisational value net is a daunting task. If done as part of an Enterprise Architecture effort, it will tend to divert the focus away from alignment and validation. It also has the strong potential for impeding the important cross-business area collaboration processes critical to the overall successful definition and implementation of the enterprise architecture.

This is not to say that a complete enterprise architectural description of the various solutions is not valuable, but rather to say that their comprehensive definition is better done outside the scope of the Enterprise Architecture effort. The level of enterprise architectural detail within the Enterprise Architecture should be governed by the overall objectives of achieving collaboration, alignment, validation and the ability to implement and assess risk:

Business Layer Definition: Business structures, relations, tasks and activities should be defined to the level of detail for which their performance metrics can be validated and their technology support needs identified.

Information Layer Definition: This activity defines key information flows and characteristics within a business area at a level of detail that can be used to access their affinities and properly align them in the overall enterprise architecture, and provide a description of information movement and security services required from the information-systems and technology infrastructure.

Information-Systems Layer Definition: Level of detail is derived from the business and information layer definition effort, which defines the required solution structure set, functions, features and standards.

Technology Infrastructure Layer: This layer defines the technology services provided, not how they are implemented.

The above level of detail is *enough*[4] to develop a holistic Enterprise Architecture that leads to the proper alignment, validation and implementation of changing business strategies, tasks and activities, information and technology. Additionally, the Enterprise Architecture elements can easily be extended on in more detailed domain specific solution architectures.

---

[4] *See the quote 'Good is good enough' in chapter 1*

5 Extended Enterprises

5.1 Managing the Enterprise beyond the boundaries

In a world populated by value creating and value exchanging entities, often the decision will come down to owning one of three fundamental value propositions.

You will either be able to own the customer, own the content that the customer seeks to acquire, or own the infrastructure that allows the content to be produced or the value to be exchanged.

Each has a different business model. Each exploits a unique core competence. Each employs a different means of generating added value. However, in the connected economy, attempting to own all of them simultaneously will increasingly become a game of diminishing returns. When the network allows competitors to fill the gaps in their offerings at no additional cost, owning all of these competencies only increases risk without necessarily increasing returns.

As the factors that make up the economic environment change under the influence of the Internet or economic circumstances, we can begin to anticipate how and where they will alter the cohesion and boundaries of the entities that make up the connected economy. We can estimate which industries and business models will likely become threatened and which will likely survive.

In the process, we can redefine the way in which our organisations will participate and continue to create value for customers and shareholders alike. In the technology, we choose the possibilities that fit best to this collaborative environment.

5.2   *The Extended Enterprise*

Within the decade, we will see highly intelligent enterprises come to dominate their space. As noted, they will capitalize on the technology to withstand shocks and to maximize fit with the environment.

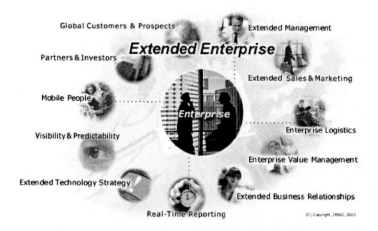

They will utilize their adaptiveness to shape and execute real-time strategic options. Make no mistake - these will not be simply "learning organisations" - but instead action-based entities that attack open space, defend instinctively, and anticipate possibilities. For organisations that do not upgrade their capabilities to competitively adaptive levels, difficulties will multiply rapidly.

Costs will appear out of control vis-à-vis the best-evolving players and historical knowledge of customers will quickly decay in value. In defence, the smarter of these players will elect to outsource large pieces of their core businesses to superior firms and then recombine the pieces imaginatively to suit specific opportunities - thus creating a modular or plug-and-play capability that is both strong and flexible and that extends their original boundaries.

5.2.1   Fundamental Structures

There are three fundamental structures that govern the nature of all economic activity: supply, demand and the way in which value is exchanged between them. At its most rudimentary level, the entire economy can be viewed as a universe made up of just these three elements: value producing: value consuming: and value exchanging entities.

However, the ways in which each of these elements is constituted, and how each relates to the others, are not fixed. In fact, these entities change their boundaries and behaviours based on a number of different circumstances.

While most organisations would readily subscribe to the idea that supply influences demand, we're not nearly as comfortable with the idea that the way in which value is exchanged influences supply, or that the way in which transactions occur can influence demand. The connected economy, as a signalling, coordination and value-exchange mechanism, is reshaping the fundamental organisation of economic activity along those very lines.

Economists have long debated the underlying principles that give rise to the overall structure of the economy.

5.2.2   Economic Models

While there are many different models that attempt to explain the natural organisation of economic activity, the Internet has brought three dominant economic organisational forms into prominent and stark relief: hierarchies, networks and collaborative value webs.

It is well understood that each of these forms becomes a preferred economic structure under certain conditions. Here are some rules of thumb:

Hierarchies (Industrial Enterprises) form when a concentration of specialized knowledge or assets is required to produce and market a product - for example how to locate, extract and refine oil.

Networks (Rebuilding Enterprises) of suppliers predominate when demand for a given product or service becomes highly specific and highly uncertain.

Collaborative Value Nets, (Extended Enterprises) emerge based on the numbers of relations (e.g. buyers and suppliers), the cost to exchange value, and the needs of participants to obtain and exploit information.

Since most economies have lengthy histories, most have also built up legacy structures. For most of the industrialized world, hierarchies make up the dominant economic pattern. However, the adoption of the Internet, with its ubiquity, transparency and speed, has begun to influence the circumstances that determine how and where each of these forms will be successful in the future.

The evolution of the organisation of economic activity is being driven by a change in environmental circumstances: the rapid exploration of the Internet and new technologies. Its speed, ubiquity and transparency are propelling the natural selection of organisation forms into specialized value-producing and value-exchanging entities.

It is certainly understandable to lament the condition that we find ourselves in across the globe, but market fluctuations are not new – nor are the threat of recession.

5.2.3 Stability

What is different, however, is the degree of volatility that we are witnessing. It seems *permanent*, if that is possible. In other words, it seems that we are in an era of rapid evolution of our economic entities, much like the evolution, which many other species have endured – except for the ones that we will never know. In situations where volatility is so marked, we instinctively reach for something to believe and to trust. If we do not find such a signal, we quickly lose our coordinates and our orientation.

In searching for more stability, we might ask ourselves, "What is constant?" The answer is obviously Dynamics. Dynamics and related to dynamics, Change is indeed a constant. Less often acknowledged, however, is the companion of Change – Adaptation. It is also a constant in that it takes place repeatedly and, in some situations, continuously. In Nature, we see all forms of adaptation taking place; not only biological but also behavioural learning, copying, and deploying are essential techniques for offsetting threatening circumstances.

Interestingly, the most impressive characteristic is not adaptation itself but the trait of adaptive ness, which seems to be a trait that can be cultivated and leveraged into flexible-but-strong strategies for survival.

5.3   *Extended Enterprise Architecture*

Here it is that Extended Enterprise Architecture can deliver the processes and structures organisations needs as well as the Extended Enterprise Architecture frameworks that guide the economic models, processes and culture of flexibility and adaptation.

And when we are able to implement controlling mechanism, the results of the E2A programs can be measured. New research is started by the Institute For Enterprise Architecture Developments to align E2A with the measurement possibilities of the Business Balance Score Card and the benefits of IT governance frameworks to deliver a unified view of Strategic Governance.

6 Enterprise Architecture Program & Validation

6.1 Enterprise Architecture Program

While every organisation's budgeting and capital planning process is different, and the Enterprise Architecture integration with these processes will vary, there are several critical success factors associated with a successful Enterprise Architecture implementation.

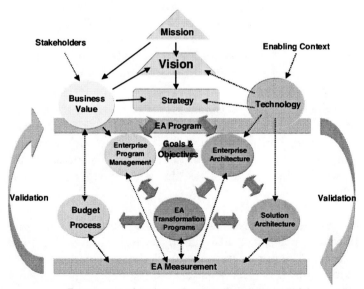

Enterprise Architecture - Strategic Governance Model

The EA implementation is funded as a separate program in itself:

o There is a budget process for "incorporating" the Enterprise Architecture to other capital programs;
o There is a feedback loop with metrics for measuring value and compliance.

IFEAD's view outlines the relationships among Enterprise Architecture, Enterprise Program Management, Solution Architectures, and the Budgeting Process integrating into the overall EA Validation, Program & Measurement Process, as presented in the Strategic Governance Model.

6.2   Enterprise Architecture Validation

6.2.1   Using Business Behaviour instead of Business Processes as part of the EA Framework

Most frameworks have business processes as an element of the enterprise architecture, when in fact a business process as an organisational entity typically has more to do with the decomposition of functions, or the needs of structuring the organisation, then it have to do with modern enterprise architecture.

Using business processes as an organising entity in enterprise architecture will most likely lead to inflexibility and fixed structures. Do you recognise the quick implementation of fixed inflexible business processes in ERP systems? It is like a foundation of reinforced concrete.

So, instead of addressing traditional well-described business processes it is better to focus on what is called 'business behaviour' when dealing with enterprise architecture.

6.2.2 Business Behaviour[5]

Business behaviour (BB) is an ordering of tasks and/or activities that accomplish business goals and satisfy business commitments. It may include manual or automated operations that complete units of work.

Business behaviour can be triggered by events in the environment or by internal initiatives or conditions. It is justified because it either generates value for the business or mitigates costs to the business.

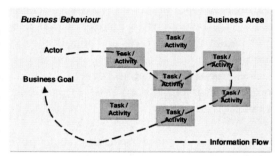

Business behaviour is what produces the outcomes that fulfil the purpose of the business. Behaviour is governed by commitments.

Actors perform it. As an end-to-end set of activity, behaviour can invoke various functions within the business. Behaviour manipulates various resources in the business in order to produce the desired result, and resources of all kinds enable it. Business behaviour is quite recursive, although various reasons and methods for imposing specific structure on aspects of business behaviour will be discussed.

The enterprise architectural purpose for understanding business behaviour stems from the opportunity to support or replace it by automated functions. From an enterprise architectural point of

---

[5] 'A Standard for Business Architecture description' by D.W. McDavid, published in IBM Systems Journal 1999.

view we are looking for structures that can help us organise the work of selecting, buying or building information-systems and create interfaces from one system environment to another and from the technology world to the world of human activity.

It is important to stress that we are talking about business behaviour of all kinds. Both physical behaviour and information-bearing behaviour are involved. We are generally only interested in physical behaviour to the extent that it is accompanied by information or provides an opportunity to capture useful information about the business. Humans perform much of the business behaviour that is covered by this concept, whereas some subset is either supported or performed by information-systems.

Behaviour can be seen as having structure by the fact that a sequence of tasks / activities performs this behaviour. Changing the sequence or the type of activities performs business flexibility. Technology has to support this type of flexibility.

6.2.3 Using Solution Sets[6] instead of Information Systems itself as part of the E2A Framework

Most frameworks have information-systems itself or applications as an element of the enterprise architecture, when in fact an application as an organisational entity typically has more to do with the marketing strategy of a vendor, or the needs of a software development effort, then it has to do with the goals and objectives of a value generating enterprise.

Using information-systems, itself as an organising entity in enterprise architecture will most likely lead to misalignment. The aspect area of Information-Systems architecture is useful;

---

[6] *Idea of 'Solution Sets'; White Paper, Interoperability Clearing House, USA, 2002.*

however do not refer to applications it self rather then to solution sets that can be supported by information-systems.

Using applications as constructs in an enterprise architectural framework made more sense in the past when there was a closer alignment between applications and processes.

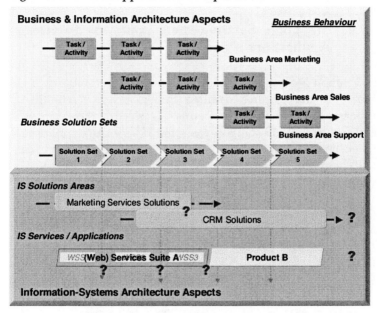

Enterprise Architecture Solution Sets

However, in the solution and package driven environment of today, it is dangerous. The misconception of the alignment between applications and traditional business processes is a major reason for the high failure rate for CRM implementations for example. CRM is a thin layer of functions and features that cross a very wide range of traditional business processes. "Architecting" CRM as a standalone application usually results in misalignment. That is why traditional business processes and applications will be no longer part of future EA frameworks.

A properly described solution-driven approach, which abstracts from the business behaviour, designs the function and feature requirements for this behaviour into "solution sets". This will result in much better alignment and will reduce inefficiencies from gaps and overlaps that result from a more typical application centric approach.

6.2.4 Mapping Solution Sets and IS Services / Applications

A Solution Set contains a description of the common required functions and features required by the tasks / activities of different business areas it supports. Translating those functions and features into IS solution areas and IS services / applications determine gaps and overlaps within existing or future products, will help the organisation in defining the best IT solution support.

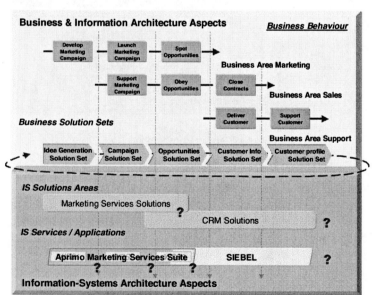

Mapping of Solution Sets

The previous figure is an example of using solution sets to transpose marketing and sales functionality and features to supporting IT solutions.

6.2.5 Alignment and Traceability

A successful Enterprise Architecture provides a mechanism for mapping business drivers to significant architectural solution areas that make up the overall enterprise model of the future state. That mapping should eliminate any ambiguity that exists about the reason for implementing that solution. The alignment also will provide the basic construct for building the business case for the solutions justification. Building the business case for an architectural solution area requires that that solution can be mapped to a business or organisational driver, and that its benefits, cost, risks, and interdependencies can be quantified.

6.2.6 Enterprise Architecture Framework Solutions decomposition

A business solution set is a part of the overall framework that is significant enough in it self to be considered from a design, costing or implementation standpoint.

Decomposing the enterprise architecture into business solutions is key to enabling the analysis process. It allows for multidiscipline teams to iteratively work together creating an enterprise view, while at the same time, dispersing into discipline specific teams performing detailed analysis and validation.

7   EA Measurement Process

7.1   *Value Net[7] Based Assessment*

Interrelationship among the solution sets can be maintained using cross-reference models, tables and matrices. Those matrices must properly allocate the benefit, cost and risk contributions of each enterprise architectural solution.

Misallocation can lead to major disasters, as can be witnessed by the mistake made by a large industry company. The industry company embarked on a $50 million plus effort to build a business-to-business (B2B) portal environment to do business transactions with their trading partners. They knew that the B2B technology was risky, but thought the risk worthwhile given the perceived benefit. The fact is that the architecture methodology used mapped the trading transactions directly to business drivers, rather than to the solution sets, it supported. The result was that the focus was on doing business transactions rather then how solutions sets can interact with each other in an extended environment. By the fact that all trading partners have their own definition of business transactions, the lack of focus on a common overall definition language was due to the result that this project failed.

A post-mortem mapping of the various architectural solutions using the prescribed structure showed that the real gains were from less risky EDI automated transactions, not from enabling the trading partners with a B2B portal solution.

---

[7] *Value Net; Book 'Architectuur, besturingsinstrument voor adaptieve organisaties' Rijsenbrij, Schekkerman, Hendrick, ISBN 9059312813,Publisher Lemma, 2002*

The logical way of doing this is to organise the various disciplined enterprise architectural solutions in conformance with their position in the value net.

7.2   Measurement and Valuation

Each enterprise architectural solution sets must include metrics for evaluating its contribution and cost to the overall enterprise value net.   Both quantitative and qualitative benefits and cost metrics can be captured for each discrete solution or product and their contributions to the value net allocated.

Business Activities

Solution Set / Cost Allocation	Total Costs	Task/activity Solution Set 1	Task/activity Solution Set 2	Task/activity Solution Set 3	Task/activity Solution Set 4	Task/activity Solution Set 5
WSS1	€€€€	%	%			
WSS2	€€€€€		%			
WSS3	€€€€			%		
Product B	€€€€€€			%	%	%

(Left axis: Technology Support — Marketing Services Solution / CRM)

Solution Set - Measurement & Validation

In the above example, IS Services / application costs are allocated at both the Solution Set level and at the Task / Activity level. Cost would be allocated at a Task / Activity level when those Task / Activities have serious cost impacts on there own, and need to be evaluated separately.

Cost and risk interdependencies would flow up. Correspondingly, benefits justifying the expenditures would flow down. So this approach is showing at the appropriate Enterprise level the individual costs spread over different Business areas. Evaluating these costs, risks and benefits as part of the EA measurement cycle at an ongoing base will deliver the validation for the added value to the business.

7.3   Enterprise Architectures: Normalized Solutions

An Enterprise Architecture that uses solution sets and normalization to analyse business needs and IT opportunities allows the development of a neutral cost / risk analysis. This cost / risk analysis allows you to understand how brittle or adaptive your chosen transformation will be.

This enables business & IT managers to see not only the benefits and limitations of particular IS services or software applications packages and standards choices. It enables them to understand the underlying risks and limitations associated with these choices: how flexible and extensible or how dependent on particular infrastructure or hardware or vendor-specific products an enterprise architectural choice makes them.

This analysis process:

1. Provides a mechanism for determining how adaptive your enterprise architecture is: Is there any one solution that's failure would bring down the companies activities? What are potential contingencies around that dependency?
2. Clearly segments enterprise architectural solutions so that they can be analysed for cost and risk. The cost and risk analysis can then be traced back to the business drivers for a comparison to benefits and added value.
3. Divides the enterprise architecture into manageable pieces facilitating its continued evolution.
4. Provides an EA framework and structure for building a knowledge base of enterprise architectural solution requirements and characteristics that can be used to

evaluate new opportunities in a continuous improvement EA program.

Additionally, normalization and solutions provides a mechanism for communicating pieces of the enterprise architecture to teams doing product and solution selection, detailed business behaviour and workflow design, or more detailed architectural descriptions that are beyond the scope of the Enterprise Architecture.

7.4 Effective Deployment via Enterprise Program Management

A major predictor of the extent to which enterprise architecture influences the actual business & IT asset base is the quality of the transformation plan. The plan factors in the competing forces impacting transformation, which typically include:
  o Potential ROI;
  o New opportunities provided by recently developed technology enablers;
  o Organisational and budgetary constraints;
  o The need to amortize existing and ongoing business & IT investments;
  o Maturity of the organisation and the capabilities of the people;
  o Maturity of technological alternatives and other implementation related risk factors.

Being able to decompose Enterprise Architectures into normative solutions provides a mechanism for experimenting with various implementation scenarios in an effort to reduce risk and adaptability.

A typical approach would be to develop a decision model containing varying scenarios, allowing benefit, cost and risks to be analysed.

7.5   Non-Prescriptive Objectivity

Many of the Enterprise Architecture Frameworks that are gaining currency today very much resemble the early phases, and, in some cases, the later phases, of a software development life cycle. This leads to a fair amount of unnecessary work and a loss of focus, as the level of specificity goes way beyond what is required at the Enterprise Architecture level. The E2A framework prevents you to drill down to this level.

7.6   Expected results from an Enterprise Architecture Program

The ultimate operational goal of any organisation is to optimise the alignment of their customer & partner needs, business strategy, organisational culture, business, people, processes and technology. This optimisation, not only provides for efficient and cost effective performance, but also helps ensure proper execution of the defined organisational goals and objectives.

However, by itself, an Enterprise Architecture program is not a panacea for success. It requires that:
1. The organisational goals and objectives are the right ones.
2. There are no inhibiting organisational, cultural, budgeting process, and people compensation issues.

These above items are beyond the scope of Enterprise Architecture. Therefore, even a fully enabled Extended Enterprise Architecture effort may only achieve incremental results, because the organisational issues presented above could limit the enterprise architecture's effectiveness.

This is not to say that Enterprise Architecture efforts are not integral in themselves, and do not bring exceptional value. However, if the hope is for revolutionary change in an organisation, a more comprehensive business concepts innovation approach, that includes an Enterprise Architecture program might be required.

7.7 *Extended Enterprise Architecture Maturity Model (E2AMM)* [8]

The table below provides the Extended Enterprise Architecture Maturity Model v2.0, describing the maturity level of implementation of an Enterprise Architecture Program.

E2AMM	Level 0: No Extended Enterprise Architecture	Level 1: Initial	Level 2 Under Development	Level 3: Defined	Level 4: Managed	Level 5: Optimized
Business & Technology Strategy Alignment	No awareness of aligning business strategies, business drivers & principles and IT strategies, drivers & principles.	Initial alignment of business strategies, business drivers & principles and IT strategies, drivers & principles.	First activities to align business strategies, drivers & principles and IT strategies, drivers & principles.	Formal alignment of business strategy, drivers, principles & functional / non-functional requirements and IT strategies, drivers, principles and functional / non-functional requirements.	Frequently reconsideration of business strategy, drivers, principles & functional / non-functional requirements and IT strategies, drivers, principles and functional / non-functional requirements.	Business - Technology cost / benefits validation metrics for end-to-end value chain on annual bus. [E2-Grid]
Extended Enterprise Involvement	No involvement of Extended parties; No collaboration agreements.	Incidental involvement of Extended parties.	Awareness of collaboration with extended parties. First initiatives to involve extended parties in the E2A program	Extended parties involved in E2A program. Definition of collaboration levels and information exchange standards	Extended Enterprise management & governance structure in place.	Measurement structure in place to manage Extended Enterprise environment
Executive-Management Involvement	E2A is not for us. We do not need to be involved. We know how to do our job. Don't tell me about	What is Extended Enterprise Architecture about? I have heard something about E2A	Little awareness by management of Extended Enterprise Architecture possibilities. Spread skepticism to adopt Extended Enterprise Architecture.	Executive management aware of Extended Enterprise Architecture benefits. Executive management supports pro-active Extended Enterprise Architectural program.	Executive management evaluates periodic the Extended Enterprise Architecture program and results.	Executive management participating in the E2A optimization process.
Business Units Involvement	Extended Enterprise Architecture is not recognized by any business unit.	Some Business Units support the Extended Enterprise Architecture program and will deliver some added value to the Business – IT alignment process	Identification that it is hard to maintain too many different business processes and supporting technologies in a dynamic business world.	Identification that an Extended Enterprise Architecture program can reduce complexity and can enhance business flexibility. Adaptive Business – IT alignment is the answer to business dynamics.	Enterprise wide business units are actively involved in the Extended Enterprise Architecture program.	Extended Enterprise Architecture is established in all business units and part of their decision making process.
Extended Enterprise Architecture Program Office	E2A program does not exist.	First roll of E2A program in place. E2A architects identified.	E2A program being actively defined. E2A program office established.	E2A program established. E2A program office actively working together with business and IT units in defining E2A value.	Extended Enterprise Architecture program office is involved in the line of business and the Enterprise budget process.	Continuously measurement of E2A program activities and results. E2A measurement, process of the overall Enterprise improvement activities.
Extended Enterprise Architecture Developments	No Extended Enterprise Architecture recognition.	Some Extended Enterprise Architecture activities are started. Recognition about focusing on business value and IT standards + cost reduction activities. Ad hoc alignment of Business and IT.	Extended Enterprise Architecture program is set up. Business and IT strategy and standards are developed and linked. EA framework and methodology are chosen but not yet widely spread.	Extended Enterprise Architecture program is established. Business & IT principles, drivers and strategies are defined and communicated. Extended Enterprise Architecture and Solution Architecture areas are defined and aligned.	Extended Enterprise Architecture program managed by E2A steering committee. Reference models are rolled out and accepted by business units. E2A program office is involved in the definition of new projects. Extended Enterprise Architecture reflects current and future state.	Extended Enterprise Architecture program office manages projects portfolio landscape and aligns continuously the overall activities and initiatives.
Extended Enterprise Architecture Results	None.	E2A results are documented in a single way. No access to the results for others.	E2A results are shared with others. Most results are documented using traditional office tools. Access to the results is limited. Sharing of information in a traditional way. Modeling and visualization techniques are developed.	Extended Enterprise Architecture results are updated frequently. Standards, modeling methods and visualization techniques are used. E2A repository is set up.	Extended Enterprise Architecture results are controlled and managed regularly. Business units are using the E2A results in their planning business. E2A results are accessible in an electronic way for all participants.	E2A results are mandatory used in the Enterprise wide strategic planning and governance activities. Continuous improvement of strategic planning and decision making cycle based on E2A results.
Strategic Governance	Strategic Governance is not in place.	Strategic Governance is in place and the first activities are set up to link the E2A program and Strategic Governance.	E2A results are part of the Strategic Governance process. The Enterprise Program management office and the Extended Enterprise Architecture office are working together on an incident base.	Strategic decision making and governance are based on the E2A results. The E2A program office is involved in the formal governance processes.	Formalized strategic governance of all business & IT investments based on E2A results.	Value measurement techniques are adopted to continuously measure the business and IT value of investments based on the E2A results and in line with the governance strategy.
Enterprise Program Management	Enterprise Program management not recognized.	Project management upgraded to program management. Recognition of the added value of Enterprise Program management. Program management executed almost in isolation.	Enterprise Program management and Extended Enterprise Architecture linked together. Enterprise Program management office responsible for the transformation part. Extended Enterprise Architecture office responsible for the Content part.	Enterprise Program management and Extended Enterprise Architecture office, officially working together. Program management approach and E2A program aligned. Accountability on responsibility of activities defined.	Project and program initiatives under auspices of the Enterprise Program management office with participation of the Extended Enterprise Architecture office. Procedures, standards and methods are aligned.	Enterprise Program Management Office and Extended Enterprise Architecture Office are participating in the enterprise strategic planning process. Measurement techniques are in place to determine the added value to the business of all initiatives.
Holistic Extended Enterprise Architecture	Awareness of aligning business and technology not present.	Awareness of aligning business and technology present. First initiatives set up to align business and technology activities, based on the Enterprise its mission, vision strategies and business drivers.	Activities are set up to continuously align business and technology initiatives. Alignment of business and information modeling methods with the technology modeling methods.	Extended Enterprise Architecture framework is used to define the business IT alignment areas. Results of business and IT modeling methods are stored in a repository. Traceability of business and IT alignment.	Every project or program initiative is measured against the added value to the business and the cost of investments. The current and future state Extended Enterprise Architectures are used as a management tool to plan transformation initiatives. Business and Technology are operating on the same level of maturity.	The holistic E2A approach is part of the organizations culture. Business initiatives are continuously reflected to the technology impact and IT possibilities are driving new business activities.
Enterprise Budget & Procurement Strategy	Separated Business & IT budget & procurement strategy.	Almost no awareness about aligning and managing the Enterprise business & IT budget and procurement strategies.	First awareness about the alignment and management of the Enterprise business & IT budget and procurement processes.	The extended Enterprise Architecture office is participating in the enterprise budget and procurement strategy. Request for information or proposals are defined in co-operation with the enterprise architecture office.	The future state Extended Enterprise Architecture acts as a blueprint for investments, is formalized and part of the enterprise budget process.	All investment plans and initiatives are related to the Extended Enterprise Architecture results, the budgets and procurement strategy.

---

[8] *E2AMM SM = Service Mark of the Institute For Enterprise Architecture Developments.*

8   Today's EA Frameworks Practice

Both industry and government all over the world have recognised the special value of Enterprise Architecture. The US government's embrace of Enterprise Architecture driven by the mandates of the Clinger – Cohen Act and OMB Circular A130, is also driven by the growing complexity of their current IT environments, and the movement from platform-based data processing into value-based services. In Europe several EA initiatives are started some sponsored by the European Union, to define EA rules for governments and in other areas of the world like South-Korea and Australia/New Zealand EA efforts are ongoing.

Industry has been motivated by the simple reality that they need Enterprise Architectures to remain competitive and support business continuity as they consolidate their long spending efforts on disparate IT resources.

While this is a positive move, a fundamental problem remains. In the rush to implement Enterprise Architectures, most current frameworks and methods are in need of updating to address today's realities.

The virtual plethora of options and overlapping products and standards, and the focus on package integration, create a much more complex environment then the environment that most of these frameworks and processes were designed to address. Most frameworks are focused on providing detailed modelling of systems and activities that are only moderately relevant at the enterprise level.   Many of these descriptive models and frameworks have their pedigree in the systems engineering arena, and so much of what is prescribed is more suitably addressed in either domain specific solution architectures or software design efforts.

This level of detail in the Enterprise Architecting effort can be a significant impediment to engaging the stakeholders effectively in the enterprise architecture team.

Finally, while most Enterprise Architecture frameworks and processes do a fairly good job at providing a means for describing current and future state enterprise architectures, and typically prescribe significant participation from key stakeholders in the effort, they do not effectively address the enterprise value net, alignment, traceability, performance measurement and the need for extended enterprise architectures that are actionable.

Enterprise Architecture

Law & Regulations

9 Enterprise Architecture in the United States Government

Largely because of the USA Clinger-Cohen Act *[CCA]*, Enterprise Architecture (EA) is emerging as a significant business - technology trend in the government sector, including federal, state, and local governments. In addition, a similar trend is emerging in industry, as companies recognise that the IT spending of the past was not well-aligned with organisational objectives, creating islands of information and systems that failed to meet their intended objectives.

Although federal EA efforts certainly do not encompass all the industry efforts to standardize and benefit from EA, federal EA efforts are important because of the large scope of the targeted enterprises.

9.1   What is the USA - Clinger-Cohen Act? [9]

9.1.1   Background

The Clinger-Cohen Act *[CCA]* assigns the Chief Information Officers (CIO) the responsibility of "developing, maintaining, and facilitating the implementation of a sound and integrated Information Technology Architecture." *[ITA]*

The Act defines the ITA as: an *integrated framework* for evolving or maintaining existing information technology and acquiring new information technology *to achieve the agency's strategic goals* and information resources management goals.

---

[9] *US Office of Management and Budget [OMB] memorandum 97-02, "Funding Information Systems Investments," dated October 25, 1996*

9.1.2   Clinger-Cohen Act sets Standards

Investments in major information systems proposed for funding in the President's budget should be consistent with Federal, agency, and bureau information architectures which: integrate agency work processes and information flows with technology to achieve the agency's strategic goals; and specify standards that enable information exchange and resource sharing.

These references highlight three important characteristics of the Information Technology Architecture (ITA) as agencies plan for investments in information technology (IT) assets:

o   CIOs are responsible for the architecture;

o   The architecture must integrate the business processes and goals of the agency with IT acquisitions;

o   The architecture focuses on work processes, information flows, and standards.

Agencies may address the topics and elements set out herein in a manner appropriate to the agency. Each element identified need not have specific or "stand-alone" documentation.

9.1.3   Information Technology Architecture Defined

For the purpose of conforming to the requirements of Clinger-Cohen Act, a complete Information Technology Architecture [ITA] is the documentation of the relationships among business and management processes and information technology that ensure:

o   Alignment of the requirements for information systems (as defined in OMB Circular A-130) with the processes that support the agency's missions;

o   Adequate interoperability, redundancy, and security of information systems; and, o   The application and maintenance of a collection of standards (including technical standards) by which the agency evaluates and acquires new systems.

The following definition of Enterprise Architecture as described in this memorandum is used in the context of the USA / Clinger-Cohen Act.

9.1.4   Enterprise Architecture Definition in the context of CCA[10]

The ITA is broad in scope and includes processes and products. An architecture in compliance with the Clinger-Cohen Act and OMB guidance will contain two elements:

o   The Enterprise Architecture;
o   Technical Reference Model and Standards Profiles.

A variety of nomenclatures used in several Enterprise Architecture frameworks are available to address these elements. Agencies may address the elements of an ITA in different ways and at various levels of granularity as appropriate, combining or reorganising the parts to create a model that suits the agency's organisational needs. Various aspects of the ITA can be developed at the agency or sub-agency level. However, self-contained sub-agency level architectures should be integrated and consistent with an agency-wide ITA.

9.2   CCA - Enterprise Architecture Compliancy

The Enterprise Architecture is the explicit description of the current and desired relationships among business and

---

[10] *In the original CCA definition of Enterprise Architecture, ITA is limited to the alignment of business requirements and IT systems. However, in later US OMB announcements, the scope of EA in the context of CCA is also addressing business & information architecture as part of EA.*

management process and information technology. It describes the "target" situation, which the agency wishes to create and maintain by managing its IT portfolio.

Documentation

The documentation of the Enterprise Architecture should include a discussion of principles and goals. For example, the agency's overall management environment, including the balance between centralization and decentralization and the pace of change within the agency, should be clearly understood when developing the Enterprise Architecture. Within that environment, principles and goals set direction on such issues as the promotion of interoperability, open systems, public access, end-user satisfaction, and security.

Guidance

This guidance adapts a five component model used in the National Institute of Standards and Technology (NIST) Special Publication 500-167, "Information Management Directions: The Integration Challenge."

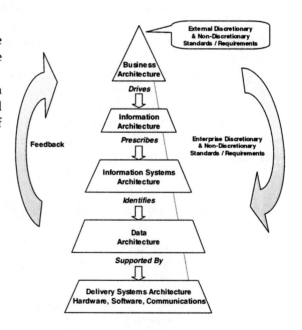

Sub or System Architectures

Agencies are permitted to identify different components as appropriate and to specify the organisational level at which specific aspects of the components will be implemented. Although the substance of these components, sometimes called "system architectures" or "sub-architectures," must be addressed in every agency's complete Enterprise Architecture, agencies have great flexibility in describing, combining, and renaming the components, which consist of:

- o Business Processes
- o Information Flows and Relationships
- o Applications
- o Data Descriptions
- o Technology Infrastructure

Current & Target Environment

With the exception of the Business Processes component, the interrelationships among and priorities of these components are not prescribed by this guidance; there is no hierarchy of relationships implied. Furthermore, agencies should document not only their current environment for each of these components, but also the target environment that is desired.

9.2.1   Business Processes

This component of the Enterprise Architecture describes the core business processes, which support the organisation's missions. The Business Processes component is a high-level analysis of the work the agency performs to support the organisation's mission, vision, and goals, and is the foundation of the ITA.

Analysis of the business processes determines the information needed and processed by the agency. Senior program managers in conjunction with IT managers must develop this aspect of the

ITA. Without a thorough understanding of its business processes and their relation to the agency missions, the agency will not be able to use its ITA effectively.

Business processes can be described by decomposing the processes into derivative business activities. There are a number of methodologies and related tools available to help agencies decompose processes (see related chapters in this book about EA tools).

Irrespective of the tool used, the model should remain at a high enough level to allow a broad agency focus, yet sufficiently detailed to be useful in decision-making as the agency identifies its information needs. Agencies should avoid excessive emphasis on modelling business processes, which can result in a waste of agency resources.

9.2.2   Information Flows and Relationships

This component analyses the information utilized by the organisation in its business processes, identifying the information used and the movement of the information within the agency. The relationships among the various flows of information are described in this component. These information flows indicate where the information is needed and how the information is shared to support mission functions.

9.2.3   Applications

The Applications component identifies, defines, and organises the activities that capture, manipulate, and manage the business information to support *mission* operations. It also describes the logical dependencies and relationships among business activities.

9.2.4 Data Descriptions and Relationships

This component of the Enterprise Architecture identifies how data is maintained, accessed, and used. At a high level, agencies define the data and describe the relationships among data elements used in the agency's information systems.

The Data Descriptions and Relationships component can include data models that describe the data underlying the business and information needs of the agency. Clearly representing the data and data relationships is important for identifying data that can be shared corporately, for minimizing redundancy, and for supporting new applications.

9.2.5 Technology Infrastructure

The Technology Infrastructure component describes and identifies the physical layer including, the functional characteristics, capabilities, and interconnections of the hardware, software, and communications, including networks, protocols, and nodes. It is the "wiring diagram" of the physical IT infrastructure.

9.3 *Technical Reference Model and Standards Profiles*

The Technical Reference Model (TRM) and Standards Profiles (both technical and security) comprise a crosscutting element, affecting all components of the Enterprise Architecture. Standards enable interoperability, portability, and scalability in systems throughout the agency. Although the specificity of the standards may vary by organisational level, the standards must be consistent throughout the agency. Standards are the basis of the development of components of the Enterprise Architecture, ultimately guide, and constrain IT asset acquisitions.

9.3.1   Technical Reference Model

The TRM identifies and describes the information services (such as database, communications, and security services) used throughout the agency. For example, Data Interchange Services support the exchange of data and information between applications. This information service would identify the various ways the agency enables the exchange of data, such as plain text, spreadsheets, databases, graphical information over Intranet/Internet, and video.

9.3.2   Standards Profiles

The standards profile defines a set of IT standards that supports the services articulated in the TRM; they are the cornerstones of interoperability. The profile establishes the minimum criteria needed to specify technology that achieves the purposes of standardization and supports specific business functions. Standards Profiles are the published sets of standards or the source references for standards that prescribe the interfaces between those services that will be standards-based. A profile may contain specifications that describe the technical standards, which enable a service, such as operating systems, network, and data interchange services.

Together with the TRM, the Standards Profiles enable the development and acquisition of standardized systems to cost-effectively meet the business needs of the agency. Agencies are expected to adopt the minimum standards necessary to support all components of the desired Enterprise Architecture. The profiles should address hardware, software, communications, data management, user interfaces, and implementation approaches, and may indicate specific products that implement the standard.

9.4   Security Standards Profiles

While security services may be considered part of the TRM and security profiles may be a subset of the standards profiles, the importance of security as a crosscutting issue warrants special attention. Security standards need not be a separate component of the Enterprise Architecture or of the TRM. Security standards profiles are Standards Profiles specific to the security services specified in the Enterprise Architecture. The profiles cover such services as: identification, authentication, and non-repudiation; audit trail creation and analysis; access controls; cryptography management; virus prevention; fraud prevention, detection and mitigation; and intrusion, prevention and detection. The purpose of the security profiles is to establish information and technology security standards to ensure adequate security for each component of the Enterprise Architecture, and to ensure that information systems conform to agency security policy. The security standards identified in the security standards profiles must be consistent with the requirements of OMB Circular A-130, Appendix III.

10 Enterprise Architecture in Europe

European Union supported projects

The European Union does not have up till know, any law's or regulations to stimulate or enforce Enterprise Architecture efforts. Therefore, in Europe most EA efforts came from consultancy and system integrator companies like Capgemini, IBM, EDS and Accenture and research organisations like IFEAD, the META group and Gartner.

The European Union is supporting and participating in several initiatives and projects, however they are not responsible for the results of these projects.

Examples of these projects are:

10.1 The InfoCitizen project[11]

InfoCitizen project aims at:

o   Establishing a common Enterprise Architecture among the participating European Union countries tested in representative public administration segments;
o   Deploying a distributed, Internet-based information system that supports the above for all actors involved (citizens, administrations, private sector), building on emerging technologies (e.g. mobile agents, middleware,

---

[11] *InfoCitizen project; http://www.eurice.de/infocitizen*

xml) and solving incompatibilities and complexities that exist today.

To achieve this, InfoCitizen employs concepts from the fields of public administration (PA), enterprise architectures and systems integration, generic process and data modelling and metadata standards (e.g. xml) in order to classify and organise information regarding a citizen/business oriented process in all participating countries.

The integrated outcome of the project, from within the appropriate preparation and launching of multi-functional organisational concepts to be developed and validated within the project lifetime, concerns the following major results:

o *Support of multi-format PA business processes* that involve interoperable information resources and co-ordinated agent application execution from the content creation level to that of content presentation;

o *Enabling of direct A2A (Administration-to-Administration) communication links* to increase interaction between European PAs, e. g. between the agents of the Citizen Point of Service usually found in a local / regional one-step shop and the various verification authorities involved which are located elsewhere;

o *Early and rapid solution to new or problematic provision of smart government services,* A2A or A2C *(Administration-to-Citizen)* based on the InfoCitizen knowledge;

o *Flexible and enriched PA communication* throughout the entire "production" process, enabling integration of the information supply chain and workflow with the demand chain (i.e. the citizen's side) and its corresponding information flow.

10.2   EU-PUBLI.COM[12]

The EU-Publi.com project introduces information technology in order to facilitate inter- European collaboration amongst Public Administration employees.

Mature and leading edge information technology solutions in the form of middleware components and Web services are employed in order to achieve interoperability. These components are structured in a technical architecture referred to as the UEN (Unitary European Network).

Amongst the important items to be addressed is the conceptual compatibility and homogenisation amongst the European Public Administrations in the areas of interest of the user partners of the project. This is attained through a Public Administration architecture that models data and processes in order to make explicit their commonality or correspondence.

10.2.1   Introduction

Governments around the world are introducing electronic government. Practically all governments are making available critical information online, streamlining their processes through the use of information and communication technology and interacting electronically with their customers (e.g. citizens, businesses). Defined broadly, e-government is the use of information and communication technology to promote more efficient and effective government, facilitate more accessible government services, allow greater public access to information and make government more accountable to citizens.

However, in order to obtain successful results from e-government, changes are required in many aspects of how Public Administration works.

---

[12] *EU-Publi.Com project; http://www.eu-publi.com*

The EU-Publi.com project attempts to introduce such changes in the particular area of facilitating cooperation amongst Public Administration employees. The cooperation that is sought in the project is defined broadly involving employees of Public Administrations in different European countries. However, the results can be applied to facilitate co-operation among Public Administration organisations, within the same European country as well as employees of a single Public Administration organisation across different departments.

10.2.2   Objectives

The high-level objective of the EU-Publi.com project is to make advances in the general area of *a common European Public Administration space*. In such a space a European Citizen will be able to request a service that will trigger processes that cut across more than one national European administration, the execution of which will be appropriately coordinated (see the macro process figure).

Currently, typical processes executed by Public Administration employees are fragments of a larger whole that is identifiable through the service it provides to the end customer (e.g. citizen). Relating these processes in terms of causal relationships, *macro-processes* can be established that typically extend over several Public Administration organisations.

A typical macro-process starts in one Public Administration organisation, the workflow then moves to another Public Administration organisation and onto a third and so on. As an example, a very fragmented macro-process for providing aid to disabled people could require up to 20 interactions with various Public Administration organisations including the Department of Internal Affairs and its peripheral units (i.e. Prefectures), the Department of Treasury, the local health authority, and the City Council.

The difficulty of cooperation among different administrations not only results in inefficient execution of such macro-processes and in the end, inefficient provision of services, but also in a frustration amongst Public Administration employees. In order to enable Public Administration employees to provide such e-government services, the EU-Publi.com project aims at achieving interoperability amongst Public Administration organisations that will allow these organisations to cooperate and collaborate more readily and effectively.

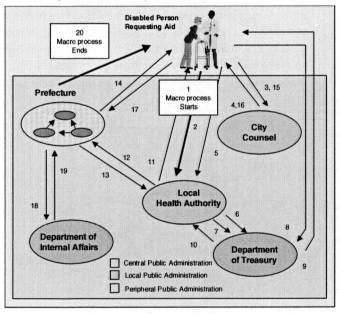

Macro Process

The EU-Publi.com project attempts to achieve this interoperability amongst Public Administration organisations by defining a Unitary European Network Architecture into which the collection of distributed, autonomous systems of each Public Administration can be brought together into a common cooperative environment. In turn, this will act as a framework for the development of new and the reengineering of existing

European Public Administration processes in order to be made suitable for facilitated cooperation.

10.2.3   EU-PUBLIC.COM Milestones

In the EU-Publi.com project, interoperability amongst European Public Administrations is achieved:

o   By building a common European Public Administration architecture, that addresses *conceptual interoperability* of Public Administration services at the European level;

o   By developing suitable software (middleware) components that will implement the interoperability features for the Public Administration domain.

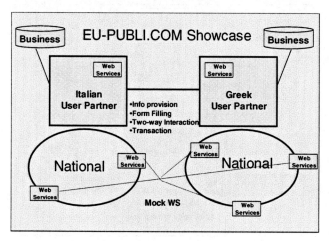

EU-PUBLI.COM Showcase

The domain in which the above will be developed in the EU-Publi.com project pertains to business lifecycle management (i.e. establishing a business, dissolving a business, providing assistance to a business etc.), since this subject area is of common interest to the project's user partners.

Therefore, key milestones of the project include:
- o The prototyping of an European Public Administration architecture in the domain of interest.
- o The demonstration of new e-services at the European level in the domain of interest. (EU-PUBLI.COM showcase)

EU Countries

However, the first individual EU countries have defined their own Enterprise Architecture, recommendations, regulations and compliancy rules. Some examples

10.3 Denmark©

On June 13 2003, the Danish Ministry of Science, Technology and Innovation published a 'national white paper' on enterprise architecture.

The white paper has been prepared by a working group with representatives from the state, the counties and the municipalities, and was commissioned by the Coordinating Information Council.

10.3.1 Recommendations

The main recommendations are:

- o The public sector - at agency level and at large - should take a more active responsibility for its own enterprise architecture.

© *Danish Government, Ministry of Science, Technology & Innovation; Source: http://www.oio.dk/arkitektur/eng*

o Government should create a joint enterprise architecture framework for the planning of government IT systems with a particular focus on securing interoperability.
o A pronounced effort to raise awareness spread knowledge and develops competencies with regard to enterprise architecture, especially around joint government initiatives.

10.3.2   Joint Enterprise Architecture Framework

The joint enterprise architecture framework should have the following elements:

o Joint coordination, including the establishing of a National Enterprise Architecture Committee with reference to the Coordinating Information Council.
o Common methodologies in terms of processes, concepts and description standards for enterprise architecture.
o Common choices regarding standards and infrastructure, including usage of a common reference profile (e-GIF) and common architectural principles.
o Common tools, e.g., by using shared databases and libraries of contract models, process descriptions, data definitions, software components and infrastructure patterns.

An increased focus on enterprise architecture and a good amount of cross-governmental coordination efforts are essential for realising the visions about eGovernment.

10.3.3   Principles

As a common architectural principle, the white paper recommends government to adopt a service oriented architecture model, in which IT-solutions are modularly designed services that have well-defined interfaces to each other and to legacy systems. In a service oriented architecture model it is a basic principle to organise components in layers that offers and uses each other's services.

Web services are a specific implementation of a service-oriented architecture.

The concept services can be understood at several levels:

o Conceptually, service-oriented architecture represents a model of loosely-coupled applications working together by exposing services to each other

o Business wise, services are expressing data- and function-services that one party can offer other parties to use, for example on businesslike terms.

o Technologically, service-oriented technology consists of a group of emerging standards that define protocols and creates a loosely coupled framework for programmed communication between different systems.

o Concretely, web services are a notion that describes a method which enables an application to be invoked by other applications by receiving and sending data in standardised XML.

The service-oriented architecture does not in itself prescribe any particular technical standards, even though several vendors offer technical solutions. The standardisation process for web services standards takes places in various international organisations (W3C, OASIS, etc.).

The white paper points out 5 core architectural principles:

o Interoperability
o Security
o Openness
o Flexibility
o Scalability

10.3.4   Structure

The architectural process should embrace the core principles. The process is seen as a double-loop process. In one loop, the main architectural process, the enterprise visions are used to define business process architecture, then information architecture, and then the technical architecture. This process defines the concrete architectural principles, which are used in the implementation process, the second loop. This process consists of portfolio planning, gap analysis and implementation projects.

10.3.5   Guidance

A Danish National Enterprise Architecture Competency Community will be established. The National IT and Telecom Agency (NITA) will act as facilitator and advisor, and host a number of community services, online and offline. NITA will also serve the National Enterprise Architecture Committee. A National Forum for Enterprise Architects will be established in collaboration with the industry and academia, and will be designed as a community of practice.

To push forward the standardisation work, NITA will present a first draft of the common reference profile (e-GIF, e-Government Interoperability Framework) soon after the white paper is published. NITA will also produce a set of guidelines.

10.4 Germany©

Standards and Architectures for eGovernment Applications (SAGA) Version 1.1, January 2003

© *Germany, Federal Ministry of the Interior in co-operation with the German Federal Office for Information Security; Source: http://kbst.bund.de/saga*

10.4.1   Introduction

With the Standards and Architectures for eGovernment Applications (SAGA), the German Federal Government is making an important contribution towards modern and service-orientated administration.

In September 2000, Chancellor Gerhard Schröder launched the BundOnline 2005 e-government initiative and obliged the Federal administration to provide its more than 350 Internet-enabled services online by the year 2005. German Federal administrations, agencies and authorities have started implementing this initiative. Since the end of 2002, more than 160 administration services have now become available online.

Coordinated by the German Federal Ministry of the Interior (BMI), an implementation plan was drafted and basic components defined.

These basic components and applications that were developed according to the "one-for-all" principle, as well as new e-government applications to be created during the years to come are to smoothly interact with each other. A uniform "look and feel" system is to be made available to users.

Following the development of the implementation plan, the German Federal Ministry of the Interior set up a project group responsible for developing concrete technical procedures for this implementation plan.

10.4.2   SAGA principles

Modern e-government calls for interoperable information and communication systems that (ideally) interact smoothly.

Simple and clear-cut standards and specifications help to achieve interoperability of information and communication systems.

SAGA identifies the necessary standards, formats and specifications; it sets forth conformity rules and updates these in line with technological progress. See for more information about SAGA paragraph 26 of this book.

10.5 *United Kingdom©*

e-Government Interoperability Framework

10.5.1 History

UK e-Envoy Publishes e-Government Interoperability Framework (e-GIF) Version 4.

The UK Office of the e-Envoy has released the e-GIF framework specification version 4. This UK e-Government Interoperability Framework "prescribes the policies and technical specifications that will act as the foundation of the e-Government strategy and help get the UK online. e-GIF version 4 utilises market driven open standards to enable the seamless flow of information from back end systems to citizen and business, and between government organisations." Through the UK GovTalk website, the XML Schemas project is defining common data definitions as XML schemas for use throughout the public sector; the website contains a number of drafts and approved XML schemas.

The v4 specification is published in two parts: Part 1 (Framework) "contains the high level policy statements, management, implementation and compliance regimes; Part 2 contains the technical policies and tables of specifications, and a glossary and abbreviations list. The main thrust of the framework is to adopt the Internet and World Wide Web specifications for all government systems. Throughout this

---

section, use of the term 'system' is taken to include its interfaces. There is a strategic decision to adopt XML and XSL as the core standards for data integration and management of presentational data. This includes the definition and central provision of XML schemas for use throughout the public sector. The e-GIF also adopts specifications that are well supported in the market place."

10.5.2   Purpose

The e-Government Interoperability Framework (e-GIF) "sets out the UK government's technical policies and specifications for achieving interoperability and information systems coherence across the public sector. The e-GIF defines the essential prerequisites for joined-up and web enabled government... Adherence to the e-GIF specifications and policies is mandatory: they set the underlying infrastructure, freeing up public sector organisations so that they can concentrate on serving the customer through building value added information and services.

The main thrust of the framework is to adopt the Internet and World Wide Web specifications for all government systems. There is a strategic decision to adopt XML and XSL as the core standards for data integration and management of presentational data. This includes the definition and central provision of XML schemas for use throughout the public sector. The e-GIF also adopts specifications that are well supported in the market place. It is a pragmatic strategy that aims to reduce cost and risk for government systems whilst aligning them to the global Internet revolution."

10.5.3   Structure

From the Executive Summary of Part 1:

Better public services tailored to the needs of the citizen and business, as envisaged in the UK online strategy, require the seamless flow of information across government. The e-Government Interoperability Framework (e-GIF) sets out the government's technical policies and specifications for achieving interoperability and information systems coherence across the public sector. The e-GIF defines the essential pre-requisites for joined-up and web enabled government. It is a cornerstone policy in the overall e- Government strategy.

Adherence to the e-GIF specifications and policies is mandatory. They set the underlying infrastructure, freeing up public sector organisations so that they can concentrate on serving the customer through building value added information and services. It will be for the organisations themselves to consider how their business processes can be changed to be more effective by taking advantage of the opportunities provided by increased interoperability.

The main thrust of the framework is to adopt the Internet and World Wide Web specifications for all government systems. There is a strategic decision to adopt XML and XSL as the core standards for data integration and management of presentational data. This includes the definition and central provision of XML schemas for use throughout the public sector. The e-GIF also adopts specifications that are well supported in the market place. It is a pragmatic strategy that aims to reduce cost and risk for government systems whilst aligning them to the global Internet revolution.

The Framework also sets out policies for establishing and implementing metadata across the public sector. The e-Government Metadata Standard will help citizens find government information and resources more easily.

From Part 2:

"A primary role of the Interoperability Working Group is to promote the production and management of the XML schemas necessary to support data interoperability requirements of the e-Government strategy. XML schemas will be developed by specialist groups, or by open submission to the GovTalk web.

The Government Schemas Group will manage the acceptance, publication, and any subsequent change requests for the schema. XML schemas that have been accepted by the group will be published and are open for anyone to make comments. The Government Schemas Group sets the design rules to be used by the XML schema developers and will use these to validate schemas proposed for publication.

The rules include compliance with W3C specifications as described in Part 2. The Government Schemas Group will track international XML specifications development through links with standards organisations such as W3C and OASIS. These links will provide provisional schemas, which will be taken as one of the inputs for government-wide consultation and adoption if appropriate."

Enterprise Architecture Frameworks

11 Creating or choosing an Enterprise Architecture Framework

An Enterprise Architecture framework is a communication model for developing an Enterprise Architecture (EA). It is not an architecture per se. Rather; it presents a set of models, principles, services, approaches, standards, design concepts, components, visualisations and configurations that guide the development of specific aspect architectures.

11.1 Benefits of an Enterprise Architecture Framework

An Enterprise Architecture framework provides a generic problem space and a common vocabulary within which individuals can cooperate to solve a specific problem. EA Frameworks are not necessarily comprehensive, but they can be leveraged to provide at least a starter set of the issues and concerns that must be addressed in enterprise architecture development.

For many organisations and technical professionals, architecture has traditionally meant an incomprehensible diagram or two that has been around since the beginning of the project and cannot be changed because "too much depends on it," nor can it be questioned too closely because its meaning is not really clear. What depends on it, and how was that decided?

The answers to those and many other related questions are too often lost in the push to meet schedules or market demands.

Frameworks can provide guidance on a broader notion of architecture than just what can be conveyed in block diagrams.

Frameworks generally adopt similar definitions of architecture but vary in their focus, scope, and intent.

Most are developed with particular domains (e.g., mission-critical defence applications or IT for large organisations) in mind. Some frameworks focus mainly on the kinds of information (e.g., types of models or data) required documenting an architecture.

Others are more strategically oriented, providing guidance on organising evolution from current to future architectures. Some frameworks also include reference catalogues of standard technology parts from which to build compliant systems.

11.2 *Creating an Enterprise Architecture Framework*

Creating a framework for an enterprise may be as simple as tweaking an existing framework or as complicated as inventing your own. In most cases, you will not have to start completely from scratch.

Even if you decide to adapt an existing framework, you still have a fair amount of work.
You will need to customize it to suit your organisational culture and vocabulary, for example.
You will also need to put the framework through several dry runs, which will inevitably generate some lessons learned.

Be prepared to spend some time refining and adding more details to the new framework because you will not get it right the first time.

> o A first step in creating the framework is to carefully evaluate and understand your enterprise business environment.

o   Second, you have to define the goals and objectives of the framework to serve.

o   Third, you have to check which existing framework fits best to your enterprise business environment and goals & objectives.

o   Fourth, you have to customize the existing framework to your needs and define the appropriate modelling techniques.

o   Fifth, you have to check your new framework through several dry runs.

o   Sixth, you have to define your lessons learned and refine the framework and the accompanied processes.

You cannot possibly decide on the framework structure without these steps. For example, most major governmental organisations are large and highly decentralized with rapidly changing business requirements. Thus, it has to be able to develop enterprise applications consistently and in keeping with the pace of its enterprise business mission.

Guidance by experienced Enterprise Architecture Framework designers / architects can speed up the development of your own framework and can prevent you from making common mistakes.

11.3 Choosing an Enterprise Architecture framework

Although there are several frameworks from which to choose and they are directed at different communities, they share many objectives and approaches.

There is value in understanding more than one framework if they add to your set of concepts and problem-solving approaches. If one framework has most of the things you need, but lacks something, identify the gaps, which you can then possibly fill by borrowing from another framework.

This book delivers you an overview of the most popular Enterprise Architecture Frameworks, their history and characteristics helping the reader in choosing the appropriate one.

The primary concerns in choosing a framework are the **stakeholders** and the **domain**.

One of the fundamental uses of enterprise architecture descriptions is to **communicate** with all stakeholders.

Enterprise Architectural views must provide information that stakeholders need in a way that they can assimilate and use. Different kinds of visualisations address different specific stakeholder concerns.

Fundamentally, the problem with Enterprise Architecture is

'Communication'

12 The Enterprise Architecture Frameworks History Overview

The history diagram below illustrates some of the historical relationships among several frameworks. Most of the frameworks represented in this diagram are described in the next chapters.

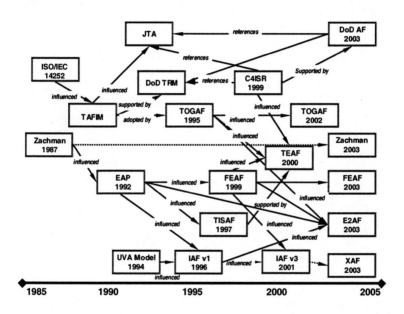

Having a closer look at this history diagram we can see that most enterprise architecture frameworks today have a common history and are build on refinements and add-ons of other frameworks.

Terminology has changed over time; however the ideas behind the function areas of the frameworks and the abstraction levels are almost the same. So, a good and experienced enterprise architect can deal with all the existing and future enterprise architecture frameworks and can tune existing ones to the needs of organisations.

13 Extended Enterprise Architecture Framework (E2AF)©

13.1 History

The Extended Enterprise Architecture (E2A) Framework is developed by the Institute For Enterprise Architecture Developments in 2002 and is based on ideas and influences of other frameworks as well as real life experience in using several frameworks.

The influences of the Zachman framework, EAP (Enterprise Architecture Planning), IAF (Integrated Architecture Framework) and the Federal Enterprise Architecture Framework can be found in this framework. The framework is the results of several years experience in using enterprise architecture frameworks.

13.2 Purpose

The Extended Enterprise business model

In a world populated by value creating and value exchanging entities, often the decision will come down to owning one of three fundamental value propositions. You will either be able to own the customer, own the content that the customer seeks to acquire, or own the infrastructure that allows the content to be produced or the value to be exchanged. Each has a different business model. Each exploits a unique core competence. Each employs a different means of generating economic returns. However, in the connected economy, attempting to own all of them simultaneously will increasingly become a game of diminishing returns. When the network allows competitors to

---

© *The Institute For Enterprise Architecture Developments, The Netherlands.* *http://www.enterprise-architecture.info*

fill the gaps in their offerings at no additional cost, owning all of these competencies only increases risk without necessarily increasing returns.

As the factors that make up the economic environment change under the influence of the Internet, we can begin to anticipate how and where they will alter the cohesion and boundaries of the entities that make up the extended enterprise.

We can estimate which industries and business models will likely become threatened and which will likely survive. In the process, we can redefine the way in which our organisations will participate and continue to create value for customers and shareholders alike. In the technology, we choose the possibilities that fit best to this collaborative environment.

The extended enterprise architecture framework (E2AF) reflects the latest developments in the area of extended enterprise architectures and supports collaboration and communication with all (extended) stakeholders involved.

13.3 Scope

Within the decade, we will see highly intelligent enterprises come to dominate their space. As noted, they will capitalize on the technology to withstand shocks and to maximize fit with the environment.

They will utilize their adaptiveness to shape and execute real-time strategic options. Make no mistake - these will not be simply "learning organisations" - but instead action-based entities that attack open space, defend instinctively, and anticipate possibilities. For organisations that do not upgrade their capabilities to competitively adaptive levels, difficulties will multiply rapidly.
Costs will appear out of control vis-à-vis the best-evolving players and historical knowledge of customers will quickly

decay in value. In defence, the smarter of these players will elect to outsource large pieces of their core businesses to superior firms and then recombine the pieces imaginatively to suit specific opportunities - thus creating a modular or plug-and-play capability that is both strong and flexible and that extends their original boundaries.

The Extended Enterprise Architecture Framework is dealing with the processes and activities of extending the Enterprise Architecture beyond its original boundaries, defining a collaborative environment for all entities involved in a collaborative process.

13.4 Principles

Extended Enterprise Architecture is not a panacea for all problems in the world of business and information & communication technology in and outside the enterprise. It serves its own specific objectives and has to be used when appropriate. Extended Enterprise Architecture is driving the enterprise to its boundaries.

The major principles of an E2A program, supported by the E2A framework are:

- o Create and maintain a common vision of the future shared by both the business and IT, driving continuous business/IT alignment
- o Create a holistic, end-to-end future-state enterprise architecture process that accurately reflects the business strategy of the enterprise
- o Build agility by lowering the "complexity barrier," an inhibitor of change
- o Increase the flexibility of the enterprise in linking with external partners

o Develop a proactive organisation capable of meeting customer demands, outpacing the competition, and driving innovation
o Reduce risk and prepare the enterprise for rapid, unplanned change
o Avoid the pitfalls of business-unit IT functions operating at odds with one another
o Institute a program of progressive technology refinement
o Create, unify, and integrate business processes across the enterprise
o Unlock the power of information, unifying information silos that hinder corporate initiatives such as customer relationship management and e-business
o Eliminate duplicate and overlapping technologies, decreasing support costs
o Reduce solution delivery time and development costs by maximizing reuse of technology, information, and business applications

To accomplish this, the Extended Enterprise Architecture approach must be:

o **Holistic in Scope:** It must address all aspects of the Extended Enterprise and directly associated with business technology alignment: business structure, Business activities, business processes, information flows, information-systems, and infrastructure, standards, policies. The notion of "Extended Enterprising" is growing in importance, and extends stakeholder status to include external value net members. Most enterprise architecture efforts are too inwardly focused, and do not include the customer and key business partners. This results in miss-aligned enterprise architectures, and lost opportunities to gain competitive advantage and government effectiveness. The "Extended Enterprising" focus directly supports

Business 2 Business initiatives, E-Government and cross-community initiatives critical to global trading and communication today.

o **Collaboration Based:** The effort must include representatives from all key stakeholders and value net members into the EA program: Business Domains, Senior Management, Business Partners, and customers. This is critical to obtaining "buy-in," ongoing support and business / partner, customer alignment and collaboration.

o **Alignment Driven:** It must address the need to directly align 'extended' business and technology drivers in a way that is comprehensible and transparent to all key stakeholders, with a continued process of tracing enterprise architecture initiatives to the business strategy.

o **Value Driven:** It must provide mechanisms to define business cases that help ensure and demonstrate the business value of enterprise architecture solutions.

o **Dynamic Environments:** It must include analytical methods that support the development of extended enterprise architectures that are flexible and dynamic to changing business drivers, new opportunities or roadblocks, and enterprise architectures that provide transformation options that mitigate risks and are flexible and dynamic to budget and other organisational constraints.

o **Normative Results:** It must provide the ability to define solution sets that can be measured, validated and mapped to real world solutions.

o **Non-Prescriptive:** It must not presume an implementation approach. That is out of the scope of the enterprise architecture program.

13.5 Structure

The E2A Framework is a clear concept with powerful implications. By understanding any particular aspect of an organisation at any point in its evolution, enterprise architects construct a tool that can be very useful in making decisions about changes or extensions.

The framework contains 4 rows and 6 columns yielding 24 unique cells or aspect levels.

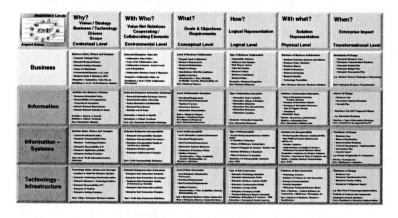

Extended Enterprise Architecture Framework (E2AF)

13.5.1 Separation of Concerns

'Separation of concerns' allow us to deal with conflict of interest between these concerns. We distinguish six main levels of concern within extended enterprise architecture studies often called levels of abstraction:

o *The Contextual level*, describing the extended context of the organisation and the scope of the enterprise architecture study. **Why**; Describes the motivations of the enterprise. This reveals the enterprise mission, vision and scope and the business & technology drivers.

o *The Environmental level*, describing the formal extended business relations and the related information flows. **With Who**; Represents the business & technology relationships within the extended enterprise. The type of collaboration. The design of the extended enterprise organisation has to do with the value proposition in the net and the structure of governance within the extended enterprise.

o *The Conceptual level*, addressing the Requirements. **What**; Describes the goals and objectives and the requirements of the enterprise entities involved in each aspect area of the enterprise.

o *The Logical level*, addressing the ideal logical solutions. **How**; Shows the logical solutions within each aspect area.

o *The Physical level*, addressing the physical solution of products & techniques. **With What**; Shows physical solutions in each aspect area, including business & communication changes, supporting software products and tools, hardware & communication products.

o *The Transformational level*, describing the impact for the organisation of the proposed solutions. **When**; Represents the transformation roadmap, dependencies within aspect areas, supported by business cases.

13.5.2   Decomposition of the Enterprise

The 4 rows represent the different aspect areas of the Enterprise:

o **Business or Organisation**; starting point and expressing all business elements and structures in scope.
o **Information**; extracted from the business an explicit expression of information needs, flows and relations is necessary to identify the functions that can be automated.
o **Information - Systems**; the automated support of specific functions.
o **Technology - Infrastructure**; the supporting technology environment for the information systems.

All these aspect areas have to be related to each other in such a way that a coherent set of relations can be identified. Integration of these aspect areas is a necessity for an Enterprise Architectural design.

13.5.3   Enterprise Architectural Viewpoints

Besides the aspect areas of the enterprise architecture, specific views can be created, based on specific viewpoints or themes. Examples of viewpoints are 'Security' and 'Governance'. The impact of viewpoints should be incorporated in the extended enterprise architecture results at all levels.

13.5.4   EA results

The E2A approach can deliver several results depending on the scope and the goals and objectives of the enterprise architecture approach. Visualising results to communicate and share with all stakeholders is one of the key products of the E2A approach, where the E2A framework serves as a guide for all stakeholders involved.

13.6 Guidance

Extracted from the E2A framework an Extended Enterprise Architecture approach can be defined to deal with the goals & objectives of the organisation.

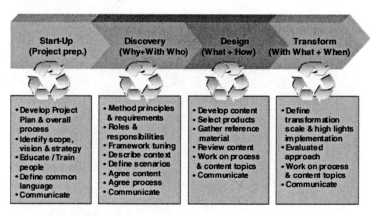

Most of the prescriptive guidance is given through publications and supporting services.

13.7 Compliance

The Extended Enterprise Architecture Framework is a standard written by an Enterprise Architecture professional institute. The E2A framework can be used to deal with several compliance rules of different organisations. However, if the extended enterprise architecture framework is used in its entirety, and all the given relationship rules are followed, then compliance for example for CCA can be assumed by default.

14 Enterprise Architecture Planning (EAP)©

14.1 History

This commercial methodology is a specific attempt to provide guidance for specifying the top two rows of the Zachman Framework: Scope (Planner) and Business Model (Owner). Published in 1992, the methodology has a business data-driven approach intended to ensure quality information systems by emphasizing the definition of a stable business model, data dependencies defined before system implementation, and the order of implementation activities based on the data dependencies.

14.2 Purpose

EAP defines a process for enterprise architects that emphasizes interpersonal skills and techniques for organising and directing enterprise architecture projects, obtaining management commitment, presenting the plan to management, and leading the organisation through the transition from planning to implementation.

14.3 Scope

EAP covers only the first two rows of the Zachman Framework. This means that only the business planning is detailed, and no attention is given to technical design or implementation. EAP has been mainly used in business and industrial information systems.

© *Spewak, Steven H.; Book 'Enterprise Architecture Planning', New York: John Wiley & Sons; 1992*

14.4 Principles

The major principles that guide the application of the EAP framework include:

- o Enterprise data should be accessible whenever and wherever it is needed.
- o Information systems should adapt to meet the needs of changing business needs.
- o High data integrity and standards should exist across the enterprise.
- o All enterprise data systems should be integrated.

These critical success factors should be obtainable cost-effectively.

14.5 Structure

The organisation of EAP is shown in the Components figure. Each block represents a phase of the process that focuses on how to define the associated architectures and development plans.

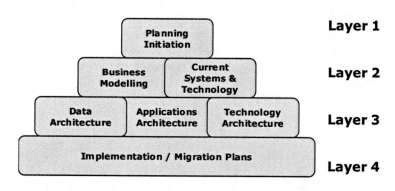

Components of EAP

- o *Layer 1* represents project initiation. These activities determine an appropriate specific methodology; decide who should be involved, and which toolset to use. With this information collected, a work plan can be written and management buy-in can be sought.

o *Layer 2* builds a knowledge base of the business processes and required information. The current systems baseline is also captured here. The baseline includes an inventory of application systems, data, and technology platforms.

o *Layer 3* plans the future architecture. This includes defining the data architecture by understanding the major kinds of data needed by the business. The application architecture defines the major kinds of application needed to manage the data and support business processes. The technology architecture identifies the technology platforms needed to create an environment for the data and application architectures.

o *Layer 4* addresses the implementation. This includes defining the sequence for implementing applications, creating a schedule for implementation, preparing a cost/benefit analysis, and defining a road map for migrating from the current state to the desired state.

14.6 Guidance

EAP is described in a book (Steven Spewak, 1992) that provides detailed guidance for the EAP process activities.

In addition to defining the roles and responsibilities for each phase, the component tasks are defined with specific guidance for their completion along with definitions of the deliverables that need to be produced.

Additional recommendations include suggested tools for carrying out the process steps, cost estimates for each phase, and many examples of deliverables.

There are sample function definitions, a business model document, a data architecture document, an applications architecture report, and sample technology architecture outlines.

14.7 Compliance

EAP is not a standard and does not require CCA compliancy.

15 Federal Enterprise Architecture Framework (FEAF)©

15.1 History

Following the industry trend of defining architectural frameworks to guide the development of large, complex systems development and acquisition efforts, the United States of America Congress passed the Clinger-Cohen Act (also known as the ITMRA) in 1996, which requires USA Federal Agency Chief Information Officers to develop, maintain, and facilitate integrated systems architectures.

The Federal Enterprise Architecture Framework is developed by: the USA Chief Information Officers Council. The USA CIO Council published version 1.1 of the FEAF in 1999.

Based on the earlier investments in FEAF, on February 6, 2002 the development of a Federal Enterprise Architecture (FEA) was commenced. Led by OMB, the purpose of this effort is to identify opportunities to simplify processes and unify work across the agencies and within the lines of business of the Federal Government. The outcome of this effort will be a more citizen-centred, customer-focused government that maximizes technology investments to better achieve mission outcomes.

15.2 Purpose

The USA Office of management & Budget [OMB] requires that agency information systems investments be consistent with USA Federal, Agency, and Bureau architectures.

© *USA Chief Information Officers Council, FEAF version 1.1; 1999.*

The overriding goal is to improve interoperability within the United States Government by creating one Federal Enterprise Architecture (FEA). The FEA would integrate the separate architectures of the various Federal Agencies. In support of this goal, the Government needs a collaboration tool for collecting and storing common architecture information.

The Federal Enterprise Architecture Framework *[FEAF]* is the current version of that tool and allows the Federal Government to:

o   Organise Federal information for the entire Federal Government;
o   Promote information sharing among Federal organisations;
o   Help Federal organisations develop their architectures;
o   Help Federal organisations quickly develop their IT investment processes;
o   Serve customer needs better, faster, and more cost-effectively.

15.3 Scope

The scope of application for the FEAF includes all organisations throughout the Federal Government and all their partners, including:

o   Large, major Federal Departmental systems;
o   Departmental Sub agency and Bureau systems;
o   Other Federal Agency systems;
o   Systems where substantial Federal investments are involved with international, State, or local Governments.

15.4 *Principles*

Architectural principles should represent fundamental requirements and practices believed to be good for the organisation, for example:

o Architectures must be appropriately scoped, planned, and defined based on the intended use;

o Architectures must be compliant with the law as expressed in legislative mandates, executive orders, Federal regulations, and other Federal guidelines;

o Architectures should facilitate change;

o Architectures set the interoperability standard;

o Architectures provide access to information but must secure the organisation against unauthorized access;

o Architectures must comply with the USA Privacy Act of 1974;

o Enterprise architectures must reflect the Agency's strategic plan;

o Enterprise architectures coordinate technical investments and encourage the selection of proven technologies;

o Architectures continuously change and require transition;

o Architectures provide standardized business processes and common operating environments;

o Architecture products are only as good as the data collected from subject matter experts and domain owners;

o Architectures minimize the burden of data collection, streamline data storage, and enhance data access;

o Target architectures should be used to control the growth of technical diversity.

15.5 Structure

FEAF partitions a given architecture into business, data, applications, and technology architectures (see the FEAF structure diagram). The FEAF currently includes the first three columns of the Zachman Framework and the EAP.

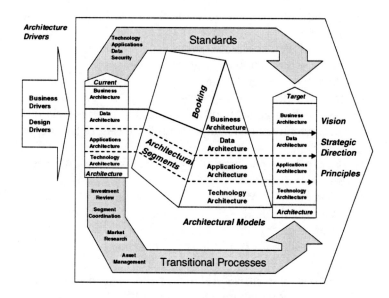

The FEAF Structure & methodology

The major components of the FEAF are:

o **Architecture Drivers.** Represent external stimuli that cause the FEA to change;

o **Strategic Direction.** Ensures that changes are consistent with the overall Federal direction;

o **Current Architecture.** Represents the current state of the enterprise. Full characterization may be significantly beyond its worth and maintenance;

o **Target Architecture.** Represents the target state for the enterprise within the context of the strategic direction;

o **Transitional Processes.** Apply the changes from the current architecture to the target architecture in compliance with the architecture standards, such as various decision-making or governance procedures, migration planning, budgeting, and configuration management and engineering change control;

o **Architectural Segments.** Focus on a subset or a smaller enterprise within the total Federal Enterprise;

o **Architectural Models.** Provide the documentation and the basis for managing and implementing changes in the Federal Enterprise;

o **Standards.** Include standards (some of which may be made mandatory), voluntary guidelines, and best practices, all of which focus on promoting interoperability.

Another view of the FEAF is shown in the alternate view diagram.

	Data Architecture	Application Architecture	Technology Architecture
Planner Perspective	List of Business Objects	List of Business Processes	List of Business Locations
Owner Perspective	Semantic Model	Business Process Model	Business Logistic Systems
Designer Perspective	Logical Data Model	Application Architecture	System Geographic Deployment Architecture
Builder Perspective	Physical Data Model	Systems Design	Technology Architecture
Subcontractor Perspective	Data Dictionary	Programs	Network Architecture

The FEAF Structure Alternate View

15.6 Guidance

The FEAF guide focuses on the processes, products, and roles and responsibilities of developing an enterprise architecture with the FEAF. While the guide addresses the enterprise life cycle, it focuses on how the FEA processes relate to enterprise engineering, program management, and capital planning and investment control processes.

15.6.1 What is the Federal Enterprise Architecture (FEA)[13]

To facilitate efforts to transform the Federal Government to one that is citizen-centred, results-oriented, and market-based, the Office of Management and Budget (OMB) is developing the Federal Enterprise Architecture (FEA), a business-based framework for Government-wide improvement.

The FEA is being constructed through a collection of interrelated "reference models" designed to facilitate cross-agency analysis and the identification of duplicative investments, gaps, and opportunities for collaboration within and across Federal Agencies.

These models are defined as:
- o   Performance Reference Model (PRM)
- o   Business Reference Model (BRM) v2.0
- o   Service Component Reference Model (SRM)
- o   Data and Information Reference Model (DRM)
- o   Technical Reference Model (TRM)

15.6.2 A Business-driven Approach

In contrast to many failed "architecture" efforts in the past, the FEA is entirely business-driven. Its foundation is the Business Reference Model, which describes the government's Lines of Business and its services to the citizen independent of the agencies and offices involved. This business-based foundation

---

[13] *Federal Enterprise Architecture Program Office; http://www.feapmo.gov*

provides a common framework for improvement in a variety of key areas:

o   Budget Allocation
o   Horizontal and Vertical Information Sharing
o   Performance Measurement
o   Budget / Performance Integration
o   Cross-Agency Collaboration
o   E-Government
o   Component-Based Architectures
o   And more...

15.7 Compliancy

The Federal Chief Information Officer has issued an executive policy to ensure that all Federal Agencies apply minimal EA procedures in compliancy with the CCA. The policy states that the EA policy within every Federal Agency should include:

o   Description of the purpose and value of an EA;
o   Description of the relationship of the EA to the Agency's strategic vision and plans;
o   Description of the relationship of the EA to capital planning, enterprise engineering, and program management;
o   Translation of business strategies into EA goals, objectives, and strategies;
o   Commitment to develop, implement, and maintain an EA;
o   Identification of EA compliance as one criterion for new and ongoing investments;
o   Overview of an enforcement policy;
o   Security practices to include certification and accreditation;
o   Appointment of the Chief Architect and establishment of an EA Core Team;
o   Establishment of the Enterprise Architecture Program Management Office [EAPMO];

o Establishment of the Enterprise Architecture Executive Steering Committee [EAESC].

Within the guidelines of this policy, each Federal Agency defines an Enforcement Policy specific to their needs. The Agency's EA processes and procedures implement the Executive EA Policy, while the Enforcement Policy defines the standards and process for determining the compliance of systems or projects to the FEAF and for resolving the issues of non-compliance.

The Enforcement Policy should answer the following questions:

o How and when will projects submit project plans to be reviewed for EA compliance?
o Who will be responsible for compliance assessment and/or justification of waivers?
o How will compliance and non-compliance be documented and reported?
o How will outstanding issues of non-compliance be resolved and/or waivers be processed and approved?
o Who will be responsible for processing, authorizing, and reassessing waivers?
o What will be the content and format of waiver submissions?
o If a waiver is granted, how will projects achieve compliance in the future?
o What are the ramifications if a noncompliant project is not granted a waiver (e.g., funding and/or deployment restrictions)?

The processes and procedures should allow for exceptions. In many cases, existing systems in the operations and maintenance phase should be granted exceptions or waivers from the technical standards and constraints of the EA. Alignment of some legacy systems with new standards could be unreasonably costly and introduce additional risk to the business users.

16 Treasury Enterprise Architecture Framework (TEAF)©

16.1 History

TEAF is derived from an earlier US Treasury model, *[TISAF]* (1997), and the US FEAF (1999).

Additional direction was provided by the Information Technology Management Reform Act *[ITMRA]*, also known as the Clinger-Cohen Act of 1996, and the Government Performance and Results Act *[GPRA]* of 1993.

16.2 Purpose

One of the requirements of the US Clinger-Cohen Act is the development of enterprise architecture (EA) in Federal agencies. Section 5125 requires that agencies develop "a sound and integrated information technology architecture." Furthermore, the OMB budget process requires that agencies indicate the compliance of IT initiatives with an agency architecture on Exhibit 300B, budget request form. In accordance with this, the Department of Treasury developed and published an EA framework in July 2000. Based on this Treasury Enterprise Architecture Framework (TEAF), Treasury Bureaus are developing architecture descriptions. The Department of the Treasury anticipates that these architecture descriptions will contribute to business and IT strategic thinking, to the integration of systems, and to the development of standards, among other benefits. The Department of the Treasury is

---

© *US - Department of the Treasury; Source: TEAF version 1.0 2000; http://www.ustreas.gov/offices/management/cio/teaf/*

developing and managing a comprehensive and integrated Departmental EA, which includes a transition plan that provides enterprise solutions.

As stated in TEAF Version 1.0, July 2000, the purpose of this architecture framework is to:

- o Provide guidance for Treasury Enterprise Architecture development and management;
- o Satisfy OMB and other Federal requirements;
- o Support Treasury Bureaus and offices with the implementation of their architectures based on strategic planning;
- o Show the benefits of incorporating enterprise architecture disciplines and tools into normal business operations;
- o Provide a structure for producing an EA and managing EA assets.

16.3 Scope

The TEAF is to guide the planning and development of enterprise architectures in all bureaus and offices of the Treasury Department. The responsibility for ensuring this action falls on the office of the Treasury CIO.

16.4 Principles

The major principles that guide the application of the TEAF include:

- o Compliance with applicable laws, orders, and regulations is required;
- o Business objectives must be defined before building IT solutions;
- o Total business value is the primary goal that drives IT decisions;

o EA is an integral part of the Investment Management Process;
o Architectural decisions shall maximize interoperability and reusability;
o Standardization will be used to fulfil common requirements and provide common functions;
o Collaboration among Treasury IT organisations will facilitate sharing the information, data, and infrastructure required by the business units;
o COTS technology will be used, where appropriate, rather than customized or in-house solutions;
o Information and infrastructure are vital assets that must be managed, controlled, and secured;
o EA must be consistent with departmental guidance and strategic goals.

16.5 Structure

TEAF has three major parts: a definition of the framework; a set of activities that guide architecture planning and implementation; and a set of guidelines that support strategic planning, EA management, EA implementation approach, and building a repository for EA products.

The framework contains resources and work products that guide EA development. The EA description must depict various perspectives of the Treasury from several different views. For instance, the Planner perspective must contain models that describe the enterprise functions, information, organisation, and infrastructure from the perspective of the executives responsible for planning the work of the Treasury bureaus and offices. Similar models must be created for the perspectives of the Owner, Designer, and Builder. See reference model.

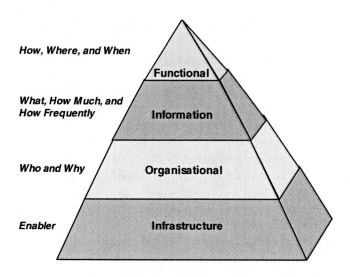

How, Where, and When — Functional

What, How Much, and How Frequently — Information

Who and Why — Organisational

Enabler — Infrastructure

TEAF Reference Model

The activities within the EA development process include:

o   Defining an EA strategy;
o   Defining an EA management process;
o   Defining an EA approach;
o   Developing the EA repository.

Building an EA repository should include:

o   Instruction on how to select information products for populating the repository;
o   Guidance on prioritising and organising the information products;
o   Essential work products based on the TEAF examples;
o   Assessments of the extent to which the bureaus and offices are using the contents of the EA.

16.6 Guidance

Although specific guidance is given for what should be in an EA, including strategy, work products, roles, and responsibilities, the TEAF leaves to each bureau the responsibility for choosing the how, when, and why. This allows each bureau to choose their own methodologies, set their own time schedule, and define their own requirements.

The TEAF provides specific guidance for the following:

o   Creating an enterprise architecture strategy;
o   Defining a road map for development;
o   Defining roles and responsibilities of participants;
o   Creating policies for configuration management;
o   Managing investments;
o   Creating an enterprise repository;
o   Creating specific work products.

16.7 Compliance

The TEAF standard provides the following advice: "A bureau will be considered compliant with the TEAF when it can demonstrate that the bureau adheres to its EA Roadmap and that gaps, if any, are not significant".

A bureau will establish a compliance/waiver process for examining proposed projects or decisions to ensure compliance with its own EA.

Compliance within a bureau can be governed separately for different aspects of the EA. Technical compliance reflect adherence to the bureau's Standards Profile. Business alignment reflects that a proposed project fulfils a targeted or transitional business need. A compliance assessment should be performed for projects of significance, based on defined compliance factors."

CCA Compliancy can be achieved when using TEAF in line with the CCA compliancy rules.

17 The Open Group Architecture Framework (TOGAF)©

17.1 *History*

Developed by the Open Group in 1995, this architectural framework was based on the TAFIM, developed by the DoD.

TOGAF Version 8 is a superset of the well-established framework represented by TOGAF Version 7. Version 8 uses the same underlying method for developing IT architectures that was evolved, with a particular focus on Technical Architectures, in the Versions of TOGAF up to and including Version 7.

However, Version 8 applies that architecture development method to the other domains of an overall Enterprise Architecture - the Business Architecture, Data Architecture, and Application Architecture, as well as the Technical Architecture.

17.2 *Purpose*

[TOGAF] intends to provide a practical, freely available, industry standard method of designing an EA, leveraging all relevant assets in the process. TOGAF is supported by a number of different architecture consultants, and it is sufficient for an organisation to use "as-is" or to adapt as an EA development method for use with other deliverables-focused frameworks.

TOGAF focuses on mission-critical business applications that will use open systems building blocks. The framework embodies

---

© *The Open Group; source: TOGAF version 8 Enterprise Edition;*
http://www.opengroup.org/architecture/togaf/

the concept of the Enterprise Architecture Continuum (described in Part III of the definition), to reflect different levels of abstraction in an architecture development process. It provides a context for the use of multiple frameworks, models, and architecture assets in conjunction with the TOGAF Architecture Development Method.

17.3 Scope

The scope of application for TOGAF includes any organisation whose:
- o Products and services are in the business and industry domains;
- o Technical infrastructure is based on open systems building blocks;
- o Definition of EA includes:
  - o Business Process architecture
  - o Applications Architecture
  - o Data Architecture
  - o Technology Architecture

17.4 Principles

Rather than providing a set of architecture principles, TOGAF explains the rules for developing good principles. Principles may be defined at three levels:
- o Enterprise principles to support business decision making across the entire Enterprise;
- o IT principles guide use of IT resources across the enterprise;
- o Architecture principles govern the architecture development process and the architecture implementation.

Example of TOGAF Principle

Principle: Maximize Benefit to the Enterprise
Statement: Information management decisions are made to provide maximum benefit to the Enterprise as a whole.

Rationale: This principle embodies "Service above self." Decisions made from an Enterprise-wide perspective have greater long-term value than decisions made from any particular organisational perspective. Maximum return on investment requires information management decisions to adhere to Enterprise-wide drivers and priorities. No minority group will detract from the benefit of the whole. However, this principle will not preclude any minority group from getting its job done.

Implications:
Achieving maximum Enterprise-wide benefit will require changes in the way we plan and manage information. Technology alone will not bring about this change.
Some organisations may have to concede their own preferences for the greater benefit of the entire Enterprise.
Application development priorities must be established by the entire Enterprise for the entire Enterprise.
Applications components should be shared across organisational boundaries.

TOGAF recommends a standard way for defining principles. In addition to a definition statement, each principle should have associated rationale and implications statements, both to promote understanding and acceptance of the principles themselves and to support their use in explaining and justifying why specific decisions are made. A standard definition should include a name; a statement of the rule; the rationale with accompanying benefits; and implications of required cost, resources, and activities. See the example from the TOGAF documentation.

Architecture principles are influenced by enterprise mission and plans, strategic initiatives, external constraints such as market factors, the current set of systems and technology deployed throughout the enterprise, and industry trends.

A good set of principles can be recognised through five quality criteria:

- o **Understandability.** The intention of the principle is clear and unambiguous to all so that violations are minimized
- o **Robustness.** Consistent decisions can be made about complex, potentially controversial situations, and enforceable policies and standards can be created.
- o **Completeness.** Every possible situation that can be imagined regarding the government of IT is covered.
- o **Consistency.** Strict adherence to one principle should not compromise the adherence to another.
- o **Stability.** Principles should be long lasting, but an amendment process should be set up after initial ratification.

17.5 Structure

TOGAF consists of three main parts:

TOGAF Architecture Development Method *[ADM]*, which explains how to derive an organisation-specific enterprise architecture that addresses business requirements. The ADM provides:

- o A reliable, proven way of developing the architecture;
- o Architecture views, which enable the architect to communicate concepts;
- o Linkages to practical case studies;
- o Guidelines on tools for architecture development.

The Enterprise Architecture Continuum, which is a taxonomy for all the architecture assets, both within the enterprise and in the IT industry at large, that the enterprise may consider when developing architectures. At relevant places throughout the TOGAF ADM, there are reminders to consider which architecture assets from the Enterprise Continuum might be appropriate for reuse. TOGAF provides two reference models that may be the start of an organisation's Enterprise Continuum:

The TOGAF Foundation Architecture, an architecture of generic services and functions that provides a foundation on which specific architectures and architectural building blocks can be built. This Foundation Architecture in turn includes:
- o TOGAF Technical Reference Model [TRM], which provides a model and taxonomy of generic platform services;
- o TOGAF Standards Information Base [SIB], which is a database of open industry standards that can be used to define the particular services and other components of an enterprise-specific architecture;
- o The Integrated Information Infrastructure Reference Model, which is based on the TOGAF Foundation Architecture and is meant to help design architectures that enable and support the vision of "Boundaryless Information Flow."

TOGAF Resource Base, which is a set of resources including guidelines, templates, and background information to help the architect in the use of the ADM.

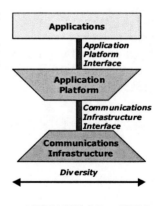

TOGAF High-Level TRM

17.6 Guidance

The ADM is iterative, over the whole process, between phases, and within phases. For each iteration of the ADM, a fresh decision must be made as to:

1. Breadth of coverage of the enterprise to be defined;
2. Level of detail to be defined;
3. Extent of the time horizon aimed at, including the number and extent of any intermediate time horizons
4. Architectural assets to be leveraged in the organisation's Enterprise Continuum, including:
    o   Assets created in previous iterations of the ADM cycle within the enterprise
    o   Assets available elsewhere in the industry (e.g., other frameworks, systems models, or vertical industry models)

These decisions need to be made on the basis of a practical assessment of resource and competence availability and the value that can realistically be expected to accrue to the enterprise from the chosen scope of the architecture work.

As a generic method, the ADM is developed to be used by enterprises in a wide variety of different geographies and applied in different vertical sectors/industry types. As such, it may be, but does not necessarily have to be, tailored to specific needs.

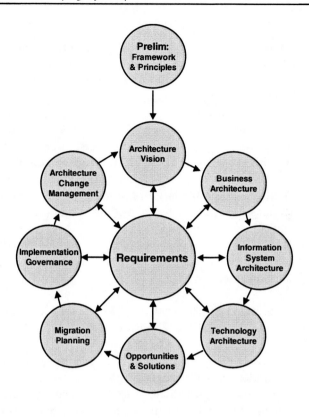

TOGAF Architecture Development Method (ADM)

17.6.1 Enterprise Continuum

TOGAF recognises the need for multiple architectures within the enterprise. These architectures represent progressions from logical to physical, horizontal to vertical, generalized to specific, and an overall taxonomy. The continuum has several benefits:

o   The Enterprise Continuum aids communication and understanding, within enterprises, between enterprises, and with vendor organisations. Individuals sometimes talk at cross-purposes when discussing architecture because they are referencing different points in the architecture continuum at the same time without realizing it. The continuum helps to prevent these misunderstandings;

o   Architectures are context-specific; for example, there are architectures that are specific to individual customers, industries, subsystems, products, and services. Architects need a consistent language to communicate the differences between architectures effectively. Such a language is particularly important when engineering systems using COTS products. The continuum provides that consistent language;

o   The continuum represents a taxonomy for classifying architecture assets, an aid to organising reusable solution assets.

The continuum comprises two parts: the Architecture Continuum and the Solutions Continuum.

The Architecture Continuum provides a consistent way to define and understand the generic rules, representations, and relationships in an information system. The Architecture Continuum classifies reusable architecture assets and is directly supported by the Solutions Continuum. This is illustrated in the figure, which shows how different architectures stretch across a continuum, ranging from foundational architectures such as TOGAF's, through common systems architectures and industry-specific architectures, to an enterprise's own individual architectures.

The arrows in the next figure represent the bi-directional relationship between different architectures. The arrows pointing left focus on meeting enterprise needs and business requirements, while the arrows going right focus on leveraging architectural components and building blocks. An architect often will look to the left of the continuum to find reusable architectural elements. When elements are not found, new requirements for these elements are passed to the left of the continuum for implementation. The Architecture Continuum is a useful tool to discover commonality and eliminate unnecessary redundancy.

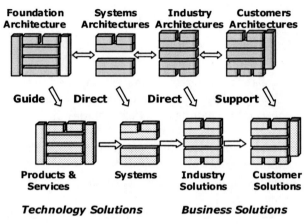

TOGAF Architecture Continuum

The Solutions Continuum provides a consistent way to describe and understand the implementation of the Architecture Continuum. The Solutions Continuum defines what is available in the organisational environment as reusable building blocks and addresses the commonalties and differences among the products, systems, and services of implemented systems. The Solutions Continuum is illustrated in the next figure.

The Solutions Continuum represents a reuse repository for the implementations of architectures at the corresponding levels of the Architecture Continuum. At each level, the Solutions Continuum is populated with reference building blocks; either purchased products or built components. A populated Solutions Continuum can add significant value to the task of managing and implementing improvements to the IT environment.

The arrows pointing right in the previous figure represent providing solutions value. Products and Services provide value for creating Systems Solutions, which in turn are used to create Industry Solutions. Industry Solutions are used to create Customer Solutions. The arrows pointing left focus on addressing enterprise needs.

17.6.2 TOGAF Resource Base

The Resource Base contains the example templates and sample procedures that provide a specific head start to architectural development. The collection of materials includes:

- o Guidelines for establishing and operating an Enterprise Architecture Board;
- o Guidelines for ensuring project compliance to architecture;
- o Guidelines for defining and using architecture contracts;
- o Guidelines for using architectural patterns;
- o Principles for the use and deployment of IT resources across the enterprise;
- o Guidelines for viewpoints and views in architecture models;
- o A fictional example illustrating building blocks in architecture;
- o A set of function views aligned with the business process structure of the enterprise;
- o A method for deriving business requirements for architecture and the implied technical requirements;
- o Real-life examples of TOGAF in use;
- o Definitions of key terms;
- o Arrangements for effective control of IT by enterprise management;
- o Other architecture frameworks and their relationship to TOGAF;
- o Strategies to ensure architecture is linked to requirements;

o Tools and techniques helpful in using TOGAF;
o Mapping the TOGAF ADM to the Zachman Framework.

The Open Group's Standards Information Base *[SIB]* is a database of facts and guidance about information systems standards. The standards to which it refers come from many sources: formal standards bodies such as ISO or IEEE; authoritative standards makers such as the Internet Society; and other consortia, like the W3C and the OMG.

17.6.2.1 *The SIB has three main uses:*

o **Architecture development.** For an organisation that is creating an architecture for its information systems, the SIB is a valuable source of information about standards that may be used to populate the architecture.

o **Acquisition/Procurement.** An organisation that is planning a procurement can use t he SIB to help ensure that the procurement gives a clear statement of technical requirements, with an assurance of conformance.

o **General information.** The SIB can be a source of information about relevant IT standards, for use by anyone at any time. The standards listed in the various tables are all Open Group standards, standards endorsed by The Open Group as appropriate for architecture specification and procurement.

The entries in the SIB are linked to other Open Group databases and resources, in particular those relating to Product Standards and Registered Products. Where relevant, the SIB also may be linked to the Websites of other de facto standards organisations. In this way, the SIB provides the architect with a gateway to a uniquely powerful set of tools for defining the standards that an architecture is to mandate and for checking the availability in the marketplace of products guaranteed to conform to those standards.

17.6.2.2 *TOGAF Support*

The Open Group has introduced certification programs for the following offerings:

o **Architecture tools**, which support TOGAF, to ensure that the meaning of a claim of conformance with TOGAF is clear and that TOGAF ADM is supported consistently in different architecture tools.

o **Training courses**, which instruct in TOGAF 7, to ensure that the course syllabus includes coverage of the necessary elements of TOGAF and its ADM.

o **Architects** trained in the use of TOGAF, to ensure that a common core of knowledge and understanding is transmitted in such courses and that architects who have completed the necessary training course and have up-to-date knowledge about TOGAF deliver professional services offered in support of TOGAF.

o **Professional services** offered in support of TOGAF, to ensure that organisations that offer such services abide by an approved code of practice and use only properly trained architects for such services.

17.7 *Compliance*

CCA Compliancy can be achieved using TOGAF when following the compliancy rules.

18 Zachman Framework©

18.1 History

In 1987, John Zachman published the Zachman Framework for Enterprise Architecture. He wrote "To keep the business from disintegrating, the concept of information systems architecture is becoming less of an option and more of a necessity." With this belief, he created the Zachman Institute for Framework Advancement *[ZIFA]*.

This organisation is a network of information professionals who understand the value of EA for organisations participating in today's global economy. The mission of ZIFA is to promote the exchange of knowledge and experience in the use, implementation, and advancement of the Zachman Framework for Enterprise Architecture. This framework is used most frequently for business and industry information systems.

18.2 Purpose

The Zachman Framework is influenced by principles of classical architecture that establish a common vocabulary and set of perspectives for describing complex enterprise systems. This influence is reflected in the set of rules that govern an ordered set of relationships that are balanced and orthogonal. By designing a system according to these rules, the architect can be assured of a design that is clean, easy to understand, balanced, and complete in it self. Zachman's Framework provides the blueprint, or architecture, for an organisation's information infrastructure.

© *Zachman Institute for Framework Advancement; Source: http://www.zifa.com/*

18.3 Scope

The Zachman Framework describes a holistic model of an enterprise's information infrastructure from six perspectives: planner, owner, designer, builder, subcontractor, and the working system. There is no guidance on sequence, process, or implementation of the framework. The focus is on ensuring that all aspects of an enterprise are well organised and exhibit clear relationships that will ensure a complete system regardless of the order in which they are established.

18.4 Principles

By defining clear architectural design principles, Zachman ensures that any tailored or extended implementation will be equally well built as long as the designer and builder continue to follow the rules.

The major principles that guide the application of the Zachman Framework include:

o   A complete system can be modelled by depicting answers to the questions why, who, what, how, where, and when;;

o   The six perspectives capture all the critical models required for system development;

o   The constraints for each perspective are additive; those of a lower row are added to those of the rows above to provide a growing number of restrictions;

o   The columns represent different abstractions in an effort to reduce the complexity of any single model that is built;

o   The columns have no order;

o   The model in each column must be unique;

o   Each row represents a unique perspective;

o   Each cell is unique;

o   The inherent logic is recursive.

18.5 Structure

The Zachman Framework is a simple concept with powerful implications. By understanding any particular aspect of a system at any point in its development, system designers construct a tool that can be very useful in making decisions about changes or extensions.

Zachman - Enterprise Architecture - A Framework™

	DATA What	FUNCTION How	NETWORK Where	PEOPLE Who	TIME When	MOTIVATION Why	
SCOPE (CONTEXTUAL)	List of Things Important to the Business	List of Processes the Business Performs	List of Locations in which the Business Operates	List of Organizations Important to the Business	List of Events Significant to the Business	List of Business Goals/Strat	**SCOPE (CONTEXTUAL)**
Planner	ENTITY = Class of Business Thing	Function = Class of Business Process	Node = Major Business Location	People = Major Organizations	Time = Major Business Event	Ends/Means=Major Bus. Goal/ Critical Success Factor	*Planner*
ENTERPRISE MODEL (CONCEPTUAL)	e.g. Semantic Model	e.g. Business Process Model	e.g. Business Logistics System	e.g. Work Flow Model	e.g. Master Schedule	e.g. Business Plan	**ENTERPRISE MODEL (CONCEPTUAL)**
Owner	Ent = Business Entity Reln = Business Relationship	Proc. = Business Process I/O = Business Resources	Node = Business Location Link = Business Linkage	People = Organization Unit Work = Work Product	Time = Business Event Cycle = Business Cycle	End = Business Objective Means = Business Strategy	*Owner*
SYSTEM MODEL (LOGICAL)	e.g. Logical Data Model	e.g. Application Architecture	e.g. Distributed System Architecture	e.g. Human Interface Architecture	e.g. Processing Structure	e.g. Business Rule Model	**SYSTEM MODEL (LOGICAL)**
Designer	Ent = Data Entity Reln = Data Relationship	Proc. = Application Function I/O = User Views	Node = I/S Function (Processor, Storage, etc) Link = Line Characteristics	People = Role Work = Deliverable	Time = System Event Cycle = Processing Cycle	End = Structural Assertion Means = Action Assertion	*Designer*
TECHNOLOGY MODEL (PHYSICAL)	e.g. Physical Data Model	e.g. System Design	e.g. Technology Architecture	e.g. Presentation Architecture	e.g. Control Structure	e.g. Rule Design	**TECHNOLOGY MODEL (PHYSICAL)**
Builder	Ent = Segment/Table/etc. Reln = Pointer/Key/etc.	Proc.= Computer Function I/O = Data Elements/Sets	Node = Hardware/System Software Link = Line Specifications	People = User Work = Screen Format	Time = Execute Cycle = Component Cycle	End = Condition Means = Action	*Builder*
DETAILED REPRESEN-TATIONS (OUT-OF-CONTEXT)	e.g. Data Definition	e.g. Program	e.g. Network Architecture	e.g. Security Architecture	e.g. Timing Definition	e.g. Rule Specification	**DETAILED REPRESEN-TATIONS (OUT-OF-CONTEXT)**
Sub-Contractor	Ent = Field Reln = Address	Proc. = Language Stmt I/O = Control Block	Node = Addresses Link = Protocols	People = Identity Work = Job	Time = Interrupt Cycle = Machine Cycle	End = Sub-condition Means = Step	*Sub-Contractor*
FUNCTIONING ENTERPRISE	e.g. DATA	e.g. FUNCTION	e.g. NETWORK	e.g. ORGANIZATION	e.g. SCHEDULE	e.g. STRATEGY	**FUNCTIONING ENTERPRISE**

(The Zachman Framework; TM of the *Zachman Institute for Framework Advancement.*)

The framework contains 6 rows and 6 columns yielding 36 unique cells or aspects.

The **rows** are separated as follows:

- o **Scope.** Corresponds to an executive summary for a planner who wants an estimate of the size, cost, and functionality of the system;

o **Business model.** Shows all the business entities and processes and how they interact;
o **System model.** Used by a systems analyst who must determine the data elements and software functions that represent the business model;
o **Technology model.** Considers the constraints of tools, technology, and materials;
o **Components.** Represent individual, independent modules that can be allocated to contractors for implementation;
o **Working system.** Depicts the operational system.

The **columns** are separated as follows:

o **Who.** Represents the people relationships within the enterprise. The design of the enterprise organisation has to do with the allocation of work and the structure of authority and responsibility. The vertical dimension represents delegation of authority, and the horizontal represents the assignment of responsibility;
o **When.** Represents time, or the event relationships that establish performance criteria and quantitative levels for enterprise resources. This is useful for designing the master schedule, the processing architecture, control architecture, and timing devices;
o **Why.** Describes the motivations of the enterprise. This reveals the enterprise goals and objectives, business plan, knowledge architecture, and knowledge design;
o **What.** Describes the entities involved in each perspective of the enterprise. Examples include business objects, system data, relational tables, or field definitions;
o **How.** Shows the functions within each perspective. Examples include business processes, software application function, computer hardware function, and language control loop;
o **Where.** Shows locations and interconnections within the enterprise. This includes major business geographical

locations, separate sections within a logistics network, allocation of system nodes, or even memory addresses within the system.

18.6 Guidance

Most of the prescriptive guidance is given through consulting services contracted through the Zachman Institute. Although no architectural development process is described in publications, there are several observations that can help organisations use the framework more effectively.

o The perspectives or rows are very abstract and incomplete near the top but become progressively more detailed and specific moving toward the bottom until an implementation emerges on the last row. This implies that the perspectives can be mapped to a product development life cycle where the top rows are used early on while the bottom rows become more important during the latter phases;

o The top two rows are intensively business-oriented and can be expressed in business-oriented vocabularies, while the bottom four rows are in the technical domain;

o Although Zachman's models are explicitly procedural, there is no reason why the representation applied to each square in the framework could not be object-oriented. A white paper published in the Rational Edge explains how the Rational Unified Process can be mapped to the Zachman Framework (de Villiers 2001);

o Business concepts from the top row must be embedded into business objects and components in the bottom rows. The business concepts can be refined over time, but their relationships should not be changed. Generic software objects and components, along with those from a specific domain repository, can be selected to populate the foundation of the system, but specific application-oriented objects must be designed and integrated to implement the system under development;

o   Because the order of the columns has no prescribed meaning, they could be rearranged to more closely follow the order of object-oriented design. The requirements are captured in the *why* column, and the actors are associated with the *who* column. Because it is generally recommended that service identification precede objects, then the *how* and *what* columns can follow. Regardless of the chosen order, note that the columns are related as in the software: the data represent inputs and outputs of the services. The *when* column can precede the *where* column if that precedence is more meaningful to a particular software development process, but the point being made is that the order of the columns can be used to facilitate discussion during object-oriented development. (Graham 1995).

Frameworks can be used recursively to manage the complexity of specifying an EA. For example, the top framework instance represents enterprise modelling of the entire business, the middle framework instance represents enterprise modelling of an independent division in another instance, and the bottom framework instance represents enterprise modelling of independent workstations.

This is only an example of how a complex problem can be partitioned into simpler pieces, while each piece can be modelled in it own right with the Zachman Framework. One framework can be used to develop the technical architecture at a level that will apply to all divisions in the business. Another framework can be used to develop departmental networks, which must conform to all constraints specified at the enterprise level. Yet, another framework can be used to develop and manage the configuration of an independent workstation, which conforms to all constraints developed at the division or departmental level.

Although the Zachman Framework is described in a very small document, the power behind the rules can be applied in many different ways and circumstances.

18.7 Compliance

The Zachman framework is not a standard written by a professional organisation, so no explicit compliance rules have been published. However, if the framework is used in its entirety and all the given relationship rules are followed, then compliance can be assumed by default.

19 Integrated Architecture Framework (IAF)
«

19.1 History

The first version of Capgemini's proprietary Integrated Architecture Framework *[IAF]* was developed in 1996 and influenced by the Zachman Framework (1987) and Spewaks ideas described in his book 'Enterprise Architecture Planning' (EAP). The current version is influenced by Capgemini's merger of Ernst & Young consulting in 2001 and combines best practices from both organisations. The version of IAF in this book is an enhanced and extended version, tuned for Enterprise Architecture.

19.2 Purpose

IAF is Capgemini's proprietary integrated architecture framework. IAF positions the way Capgemini communicates about enterprise architecture with all stakeholders, based on the philosophy and mindset behind the framework.

Every complex thing that has **to operate** as **one system** has to **be designed** as **one system**. This to guarantee integration and coherency of all its components and to ensure the system will operate the way required when it is created.

19.3 Scope

The Integrated Architecture Framework forces enterprise architects to ensure that the organisation fully benefits from the alignment of business and technology by integrating all architecture aspect areas into one overall result, i.e. The

---

* *Proprietary framework of Capgemini.*

enterprise architectural result has to consist of interlinked business, information, information systems, infrastructure, security and governance aspects.

The risk taken when not creating an integrated architecture result is that time and money are thrown away due to inefficiencies and insufficient insight in the complexity of the overall structure.

IAF	Business	Information	Information-systems	Technology-Infrastructure
Why ? Contextual	The Future, the Organisation & Environment			
What ? Conceptual	The concepts, what do we want?			
How ? Logical	Logical directions & solutions			
With what ? Physical	Physical solutions based on change, redesign, products or techniques			
When ? Transformational	Change from the existing to a future situation			
	Security / Governance		*Architecture* *ViewPoints*	

IAF Enhanced Edition

19.4 Principles

Enterprise Architecture is not a panacea for all problems in the world of business and information & communication technology. It serves its own specific objectives and has to be used when appropriate.

The Integrated Architecture framework is a communication vehicle for all stakeholders involved in an architecture program to explain and show relations, dependencies, influences and complexity of the situation of study.

IAF major principles:
o Architecture results as well as IAF itself can be used as an Atlas for management to navigate to all relevant topics;
o From IAF, roadmaps can be defined to identify the necessary tasks and activities;
o IAF can show the complexity of elements to be addressed;
o IAF can show the people to be involved in the process;
o IAF shows the relations and dependencies;
o IAF is your Guide in all Architectural Activities.

19.5 Structure

Enterprise Architecture in the context of this IAF description addresses the aspect areas required to design an integrated enterprise wide architecture of organisations and IT.

Therefore, the following main architecture areas are identified as mandatory for an integrated architecture:

o Business or Organisation; starting point and expressing all business elements and structures in scope;
o Information; extracted from the business an explicit expression of information needs, flows and relations is necessary to identify the functions that can be automated;
o Information - Systems; the automated support of specific functions;
o Technology - Infrastructure; the supporting environment for the information systems.

All these areas have to be related to each other in such a way that a coherent set of relations can be identified. Integration of these aspect areas is a necessity for an Integrated Architectural design.

The status and position of specific enterprise architecture items can change in time. For example, software developed for a specific situation can become so common, that it is used throughout the whole organisation in such a way that it actually is part of the technology infrastructure. Physical examples are the 'Office Suite' packages with common business functionality used by the whole organisation. In our terms, this type of common functionality (realised in products) has become part of the technology infrastructure.

In prescribing the structure of *an organisation and its related business* and *IT*, the architecture defines principles, guidelines and rules for:

- o The type of components of which the business or system may be composed;
- o How these components must fit together;
- o How the components communicate and co-operate;
- o What assemblies of the components are allowed;
- o What functions (communication, control, security, and information) the components and component assemblies support;
- o And how the style expresses the (cultural) values of the stakeholders of that organisation.

19.5.1 Separation of Concerns

'Separation of concerns' allow us to deal with conflict of interest between these concerns. We distinguish five main levels of concern within architecture studies often called levels of abstraction:

o The Contextual level, describing the context of the organisation and the scope of the architecture study;
o The Conceptual level, addressing the Requirements;
o The Logical level, addressing the ideal logical solutions;
o The Physical level, addressing the physical solution of products & techniques.
o The transformational level, describing the impact for the organisation of the proposed solutions.

19.5.2 Architectural Viewpoints

Architectural Viewpoint: a perspective from which to view an architecture (IEEE 1471-2000). Besides the aspect areas of architecture, specific views can be created, based on specific viewpoints or themes. Viewpoints deliver added value to the aspect areas by addressing and focusing on these specific themes, covering all aspect areas and levels.

19.6 Guidance

Most of the prescriptive guidance is given through consulting services contracted through Capgemini. An architectural development process is described in Capgemini internal publications as well at a high level in the book 'Architectuur, besturingsinstrument voor adaptieve organisaties'[14].

19.7 Compliance

The Integrated Architecture Framework is not a standard written by a professional organisation, so no explicit compliance rules have been published. However, if the integrated architecture framework is used in its entirety and all the given

---

[14] Book, 'Architectuur, besturingsinstrument voor adaptieve organisaties'; Publisher Lemma; ISBN 9059312813; Language Dutch.

relationship rules are followed, and then compliance can be assumed.

20 Joint Technical Architecture (JTA)©

20.1 History

Version 1.0 of the US Department of Defence (DoD) Joint Technical Architecture was released on 22 August 1996 and was immediately mandated by the Under Secretary of Defence, Acquisition and Technology (USD [A&T]) and ASD(C3I) for all new and upgraded C4I systems in DoD.

JTA Version 2.0 development began in March 1997 under the direction of a Technical Architecture Steering Group (TASG), co-chaired by ASD (C3I) and USD (AT&L) Open Systems Joint Task Force (OSJTF). The applicability and scope of Version 2.0 of the JTA was expanded to include the information technology in all DoD systems.

JTA Version 3.0 development began in June 1998. JTA Version 3.0 includes additional sub domains and incorporated the newly developed DoD Technical Reference Model (DoD TRM). JTA Version 3.1 mandated a Gigabit Ethernet standard. JTA Version 4.0 was available July 2002. JTA Version 4.0 removes the Orange Book mandate and mandates the Common Criteria.

The DoD Joint Technical Architecture (JTA) version 5.0 is currently being reviewed (08-2003) by the National Defence Industrial Association (NDIA).

© *US Department of Defence; Source: Joint Technical Architecture version 4; http://www-jta.itsi.disa.mil/*

20.1.1 Evolution

The evolution of the US national military strategy in the post-Cold War era and the lessons learned from conflicts like Desert Shield/Desert Storm has resulted in a new vision for the US DoD.

Joint Vision 2010 is the conceptual template for how America's Armed Forces will channel the vitality and innovation of their people and leverage technological opportunities to achieve new levels of effectiveness in joint war fighting.

This template provides a common direction to our Services in developing their unique capabilities within a joint framework of doctrine and programs as they prepare to meet an uncertain and challenging future. The Chairman of the Joint Chiefs of Staff said in Joint Vision 2010, "The nature of modern warfare demands that we fight as a joint team. This was important yesterday, it is essential today, and it will be even more imperative tomorrow."

Joint Vision 2010 (JV 2010) creates a broad framework for understanding joint warfare in the future, and for shaping Service programs and capabilities to fill our role within that framework. JV 2010 defines four operational concepts: Precision Engagement, Dominant Manoeuvre, Focused Logistics, and Full Dimensional Protection.

These concepts combine to ensure that American forces can secure Full Spectrum Dominance, i.e., the capability to dominate an opponent across the range of military operations and domains. Furthermore, Full Spectrum Dominance requires Information Superiority, i.e., the capability to collect, process, analyse, and disseminate information while denying an adversary the ability to do the same. Interoperability is crucial to Information Superiority.

Recognising the need for joint operations in combat and the reality of a shrinking budget, the Assistant Secretary of Defence (Command, Control, Communications, and Intelligence) (ASD[C3I]) issued a memorandum on 14 November 1995 to Command, Service, and Agency principals involved in the development of Command, Control, Communications, Computers, and Intelligence (C4I) systems.

This directive tasked them to "reach a consensus of a working set of standards" and "establish a single, unifying DoD technical architecture that will become binding on all future DoD C4I acquisitions" so that "new systems can be born joint and interoperable and existing systems will have a baseline to move toward interoperability."

A Joint Technical Architecture Working Group (JTAWG), chaired by ASD (C3I), was formed, and its members agreed to use the U.S. Army Technical Architecture (ATA) as the starting point for the JTA.

20.2 Purpose

War fighter battle space is complex and dynamic, requiring timely and informed decisions by all levels of military command.

There is an unprecedented increase in the amount of data and information necessary to conduct operational planning and combat decision-making. Information concerning targets, movement of forces, condition of equipment, levels of supplies, and disposition of assets—both friendly and unfriendly—must be provided to joint commanders and their forces. Therefore, information must flow quickly and seamlessly among all tactical, strategic, and supporting elements.

As shown in the next figure, war fighters must be able to work together within and across Services in ways not totally defined in today's operational concepts and/or architectures.

They must be able to obtain and use intelligence from national and theatre assets that may be widely dispersed geographically.

Sensor Grid
Connects the sensors into the System

Information Grid
Connects the Command & Control Functions into the System

Engagement Grid
Connects the shooters into the System

Today's split-base/reach-back concept requires them to obtain their logistics and administrative support from both home bases and deployed locations. All of this requires that information flow quickly and seamlessly among DoD's sensors, processing and command centres, shooters, and support activities to achieve dominated battlefield awareness and move inside the enemy's decision loop.

20.3 Scope

The DoD Joint Technical Architecture provides the minimum set of standards that, when implemented, facilitates this flow of information in support of the war fighter. The JTA standards promote:

o   A distributed information processing environment in which applications are integrated;
o   Applications and data independent of hardware to achieve true integration;
o   Information transfer capabilities to ensure seamless communications within and across diverse media;
o   Information in a common format with a common meaning;
o   Common human-computer interfaces for users, and effective means to protect the information.

The current JTA concept is focused on the interoperability and standardization of information technology (IT).

20.4 Principles

o   The JTA is used to determine the mandated standards within applicable service areas for implementation within new or upgraded systems. However, there are several key considerations in using the JTA.
o   The mandatory standards in the JTA must be implemented or used by systems that have a need for the corresponding JTA service/interface. A standard is mandatory in the sense that if a service/interface is going to be implemented, it shall be implemented in accordance with the associated standard. If a required service/interface can be obtained by implementing more than one standard (e.g., operating system standards), the appropriate standard should be selected based on system requirements.

o   The JTA is a forward-looking document. It guides the acquisition and development of new and emerging functionality and provides a baseline toward which existing systems will move. It is the minimal set of standards (for interfaces/services) that should be used now and in the future. It is *not* a catalog of all information technology standards used within today's DoD systems. If legacy standards are needed to interface with existing systems, they can be implemented on a case-by-case basis in addition to the mandated standard.

20.5 Structure

The C4ISR Architecture Framework (CAF) provides information addressing the development and presentation of architectures. The framework provides the rules, guidance, and product descriptions for developing and presenting architectures to ensure a common denominator for understanding, comparing, and integrating architectures across and within DoD.

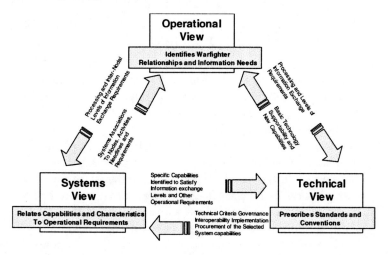

JTA Overview

DoD has implemented this by defining an interrelated set of views: operational, system, and technical. The previous figure shows the relationship among the three views.

The definitions are provided here to ensure a common understanding of the three views.

20.5.1 Operational Architecture View

The operational architecture (OA) view is a description of the tasks and activities, operational elements, and information flows required to accomplish or support a military operation.

It contains descriptions (often graphical) of the operational elements, assigned tasks and activities, and information flows required to support the war fighter. It defines the types of information exchanged, the frequency of exchange, which tasks and activities are supported by the information exchanges, and the nature of information exchanges in detail sufficient to ascertain specific interoperability requirements.

20.5.2 Technical Architecture View

The technical architecture (TA) view is the minimal set of rules governing the arrangement, interaction, and interdependence of system parts or elements, whose purpose is to ensure that a conformant system satisfies a specified set of requirements.

The technical architecture view provides the technical systems implementation guidelines upon which engineering specifications are based, common building blocks are established, and product lines are developed. The technical architecture view includes a collection of the technical standards, conventions, rules, and criteria organised into profile(s) that govern system services, interfaces, and relationships for particular systems-architecture views and that relate to particular operational views.

20.5.3   Systems Architecture View

The systems architecture (SA) view is a description, including graphics, of systems and interconnections providing for, or supporting, war fighting functions. For a domain, the systems architecture view shows how multiple systems link and interoperates, and may describe the internal construction and operations of particular systems within the architecture. For the individual system, the systems architecture view includes the physical connection, location, and identification of key nodes (including materiel-item nodes), circuits, networks, war fighting platforms, etc., and it specifies system and component performance parameters (e.g., mean time between failure, maintainability, availability).

The systems architecture view associates physical resources and their performance attributes to the operational view and its requirements following standards defined in the technical architecture.

20.6 Guidance

The main body identifies the "Core" set of JTA elements consisting of service areas, interfaces, and standards. Each section of the main body, except for the overview, is divided into four subsections as follows:

- o **Introduction, Purpose, Scope, and Background:** These subsections are for information purposes only. They define the purpose and scope of the document and the section and provide background descriptions and definitions that are unique to this section;
- o **Service Area and Services:** This subsection describes the technical overview of the Services in this section;
- o **Mandated Standards:** This subsection identifies mandatory standards or practices. Each mandated standard or practice is clearly identified on a separate bulletined () line and includes a formal reference citation

suitable for inclusion within Requests for Proposals (RFPs), Statements of Work (SOWs), or Statements of Objectives (SOOs);

o **Emerging Standards:** This subsection provides an information-only description of standards that are candidates for possible addition to the JTA mandates. Each emerging standard is clearly identified on a separate dashed (–) line. The purpose of listing these candidates is to help the program manager determine those areas likely to change in the near term (within three years) and suggest those areas in which "up-gradability" should be a concern. The expectation is that emerging standards will be elevated to mandatory status when implementations of the standards mature. Emerging standards may be implemented, but shall not be used in lieu of a mandated standard.

20.6.1 Domains and Sub domains

The JTA Core contains the common service areas, interfaces, and standards (JTA elements) applicable to all DoD systems to support interoperability. Recognising that there are additional JTA elements common within families of related systems (i.e., domains), the JTA adopted the domain and sub domain notion.

A domain represents a grouping of systems sharing common functional, behavioural, and operational requirements. JTA domains and sub domains are intended to exploit the common service areas, interfaces, and standards supporting interoperability across systems within the domain and/or sub domain.

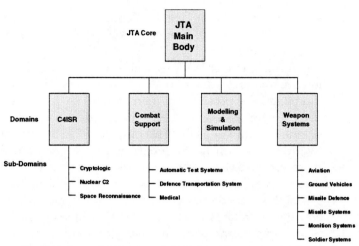

The JTA relationship between the JTA Core, domains, and sub domains.

20.6.1.1 Domains

A JTA domain contains domain-specific JTA elements applicable within the specified family of systems to further support interoperability within the systems represented in the domain—in addition to those included in the JTA Core. A domain may be composed of multiple sub domains. Sub domains represent the decomposition of a domain (referred to as the sub domain's parent domain) into a subset of related systems, exploiting additional commonalities and addressing variances within the domain.

JTA Domains:
- o Combat Support (CS)
- o Command, Control, Communications, Computers, Intelligence, Surveillance, and Reconnaissance (C4ISR)
- o Modelling and Simulation (M&S)
- o Weapon Systems (WS)

20.6.1.2 Sub domains

A sub domain contains domain-specific JTA elements applicable within the specified family of systems to further support interoperability within the systems represented in the sub domain—in addition to those included in the JTA Core and in the parent domain.

JTA Sub domains:
- o   Automatic Test Systems (ATS)
- o   Aviation (AV)
- o   Cryptologic (CRY)
- o   Defence Transportation System (DTS)
- o   Ground Vehicles (GV)
- o   Medical (MED)
- o   Missile Defence (MD)
- o   Missile Systems (MS)
- o   Munitions Systems (MUS)
- o   Nuclear Command and Control (NCC)
- o   Soldier Systems (SS)
- o   Space Reconnaissance (SR)
- o

20.7 Compliance

Relationships between the C4ISR Architecture Framework 2.0 and the DoD JTA

The C4ISR Architecture Framework defines the technical architecture view and a set of standard technical products for DoD use. The JTA is one of the Universal Reference Resources named in the CAF.

The JTA is the primary source document to the essential and supporting Technical Architecture products defined in the C4ISR Architecture Framework. Standards chosen from the JTA and other sources to meet system and operational requirements are incorporated into the technical architecture View.

CCA compliancy is not one of the goals of JTA, therefore JTA does not follow the rules of CCA compliancy.

21 C4ISR and DoDAF©

Command, Control, Communications, Computer, Intelligence,
Surveillance and Reconnaissance [C4ISR]

Department of Defence Architecture Framework [DoDAF]

21.1 History

In response to increasing needs for joint and multinational military operations, the DoD has become increasingly aware of the need for a standard architectural approach to ensure that its systems can communicate and interoperate. Beginning in 1995, the DoD has developed guidance on architecture development. The C4ISR Architecture Framework, Version 1.0 was published in 1996. Version 2 of the framework was published in 1997. After experience with these versions and in recognition of the need to strengthen adoption, the DoD is nearing completion on a new version entitled the DoD Architecture Framework, Version 1.0.

21.2 Purpose

The C4ISR Architecture Framework is intended to ensure that the architecture descriptions developed by the Commands, Services, and Agencies are inter-relatable between and among each organisation's operational, systems, and technical architecture views, and are comparable and interoperable across Joint and combined organisational boundaries.

The DoD Architecture Framework is an evolution of the C4ISR Architecture Framework. When finalized and released in late

---

© *USA Department of Defence; Sources: C4ISR Architecture Framework, version 2.0;*
DoD Architecture Framework, draft version 1.0

2003, the DoDAF will supersede the C4ISR Framework. Its intent remains ensuring that architecture descriptions can be interrelated and that resulting systems can interoperate.

21.3 Scope

The framework provides rules and guidance for developing and presenting architecture descriptions. The products defined by the framework are the work products of architecture development, the descriptive artefacts that communicate the architecture.

The framework provides direction on how to *describe* architectures; it does not provide guidance in how to *construct* or *implement* a specific architecture or how to *develop* and *acquire* systems or systems-of-systems. This framework covers the military domain and is used mainly by the DoD.

21.4 Principles

Complete architectural descriptions require the use of multiple views, each of which conveys different aspects of the architecture in several products (descriptive artefacts or models). The C4ISR/DoDAF Framework defines the following views:

Operational View depicts what is going on in the real world that is to be supported or enabled by systems represented in the architecture. Activities performed as parts of DoD missions and the associated information exchanges among personnel or organisations are the primary items modelled in operational views. The operational view reveals requirements for capabilities and interoperability.

Systems View describes existing and future systems and physical interconnections that support the DoD needs documented in the operational view.

Technical Standards View catalogues standard *[COTS, GOTS]* system parts or components and their interconnections. This view augments the systems view with technical detail and forecasts of standard technology evolution.

All View augments the other views by providing context, summary or overview-level information, and an integrated dictionary to define terms.

21.5 Structure

The C4ISR/DoD Architecture Framework contains four main types of guidance for architecture development:
- **Guidelines**, which include a set of guiding principles and guidance for building architectures that, are compliant with the framework;
- High-level **process** for using the framework to develop architecture descriptions that fulfil a purpose;
- Discussion of architecture **data** and tools that can serve as facilitators of the architecture-description process;
- Detailed description of the **products.**

21.6 Guidance

The DoDAF is organised into three volumes.
- Volume I provide general guidance on the need for and use of architecture descriptions in the DoD context;
- Volume II provides detailed definitions of the 26 products contained in the 3 views;
- Volume III is a desk book that provides examples of compliant architectures, approaches to architecture development, and information on reference resources.

21.6.1   Data and Tools

The Core Architecture Data Model *[CADM]* is a formal model of architecture products, structures, and their interrelationships. The CADM is aimed at providing a common schema for repositories of architecture information. Tool builders or vendors providing support for DoDAF-style architecture descriptions would implement the CADM with a database.

A repository based on the CADM would be able to store architecture products from multiple, framework-based architecture projects in a common way, so that products from different projects, organisations, or services could be analysed and compared.

The DoD Architecture Repository System *[DARS]*, under concurrent development with the DoDAF, is a repository for approved architecture information.

21.6.2   Products

The C4ISR and DoDAF define 26 different architecture products, which are organised into the All, Operational, Systems, and Technical views. Although the C4ISR Framework further delineated essential (required) and supporting subsets of these products, the DoDAF has relaxed this requirement to emphasize the need for developing or presenting the products that are appropriate for a given audience. With a CADM-based tool set or repository, extracting and presenting an appropriate subset of the architectural information should be at least partially automated.

A comprehensive description of the products is provided in both framework descriptions.

All View

o Overview and Summary Information. Details scope, purpose, environment, and other summary-level formation for an architecture description;
o Integrated Dictionary. Provides definitions of all terms used in all products.

Operational View

o Operational Concept Graphic. Provides a graphical and textual description of the operational concept;
o Operational Node Connectivity Description. Lists the operational nodes, activities performed at each node, connectivity, and information needs between nodes;
o Operational Information Exchange Matrix. Lists and describes information exchanged between nodes;
o Organisational Relationships Chart. Lists organisations, roles, and relationships among organisations;
o Operational Activity Model. Details the activities performed and their interrelationships, including input/output relationships;
o Operational Rules Model. Identifies business rules that govern or constrain operations;
o Operational State Transition. Identifies sequencing and timing of activities;
o Operational Event Trace. Traces actions in a scenario or sequence of events;
o Logical Data Model. Identifies data requirements of the operational view.

Systems View

o Systems Interface Description. Lists systems, system components, and their interconnections;
o Systems Communications Description. Identifies system communications;

o   Systems-Systems Matrix. Lists connections between individual systems in a group;
o   Systems Functionality Description. Lists functions performed by individual systems and the related information flow;
o   Operational Activity to Systems Function Traceability Matrix. Maps systems information back to the operational view;
o   Systems Data Exchange Matrix. Provides detail of data moving between systems;
o   Systems Performance Parameters Matrix. Lists performance characteristics of individual systems;
o   Systems Evolution Description. Lists migration plans for systems;
o   Systems Technology Forecast. Lists technologies and products that are expected to affect systems;
o   Systems Rules Model. Describes constraints on system operation imposed by design or implementation;
o   Systems State Transition Description. Describes system activity sequencing and timing;
o   Systems Event Trace Description. Describes system-specific requirements on critical event sequences;
o   Physical Schema. Describes the physical implementation of the logical data model from the operational view.

Technical Standards View

o   Technical Standards Profile. Lists technical standards that apply to the architecture;
o   Technical Standards Forecast. Describes emerging or evolving standards that will or are likely to apply to the architecture.

21.7 Compliance

In order to comply with CCA and the framework, architecture descriptions must:

o   Include the appropriate set of products for the intended use;
o   Use the common terms and definitions as specified in the framework;
o   Be consistent with the Global Information Grid [GIG] Architecture and the Joint Technical Architecture [JTA];
o   Describe interoperability requirements in a standard way.

22 Department of Defence Technical Reference Model (DoD TRM)©

22.1 History

The DoD TRM should be referenced for the complete definition of a service or interface. DoD Memorandum March 21, 2000, Subject-DoD Technical Reference Model (DoD TRM), Version 1.0 and DoD Memorandum November 29, 1999, Subject-DoD Joint Technical Architecture Version 3.0 contained in Appendix A should be consulted for amplifying guidance.

The DoD Technical Reference Model (DoD TRM) User Guide is to be used with the DoD TRM document. The User Guide provides added insight into a number of areas that are not elaborated in the DoD TRM document:

o   How to use the DoD Technical Reference Model;
o   Insight into examples and case studies;
o   Different applications of the DoD TRM;
o   How to interpret and use model service and interface categories;
o   Contrasts and identifies the relationships between the DoD TRM document and other related documents (e.g., Joint Technical Architecture [JTA], Defence Information Infrastructure Common Operating Environment [DII COE]; Command, Control, Communications, Computers, Intelligence, Surveillance, and Reconnaissance Architecture Framework [C4ISR AF]);
o   Methodology for applying the DoD TRM.

© *US Department of Defence; DoD Technical Reference Model, Version 1.0 and the DoD TRM Users guide, 2001*

22.2 *Purpose*

The DoD TRM and the accompanied User Guide is promulgated to provide knowledge and insight in using the DoD TRM to address and resolve a variety of interoperability, portability, and open system issues. The purpose is to impart an understanding of how the model provides a foundation for developing technical and operational architectures, for defining services and interfaces, and when to invoke or use a particular model view (i.e., service or interface or both). Use of the DoD TRM and the user guide promotes the development and fielding of systems that will support joint and combined operations interoperability, as well as information systems interoperability.

In the past, interoperability between DoD systems has not been addressed in a uniform and consistent manner in seeking effective solutions. The importance of battlefield interoperability and the ability of systems to exchange information is recognised as a decisive advantage in military operations and mandated in key DoD policy, regulations, memoranda, and directives: 5000.1 and .2-R; DoD 4630.5 and .8R (see Appendix A). Under revised policy mandates (CJCSI 3170-01A), interoperability has been defined as a key performance parameter (KPP), and must also be considered in mission unique systems since their products or components may be used elsewhere in the battlefield.

The model is not an end in itself nor is it an architecture. It is an aid to developing architectures and addressing a broad range of interoperability and open system issues. Additionally, the model can be used to support reuse and portability issues that are often intertwined with interoperability in the development of architectures, migration of systems, and legacy systems.

22.3 Scope

The scope of the DoD TRM is sufficiently broad to assist in addressing a wide range of problems and system configurations. The model does not restrict a user to specific system architectures, but rather supports distributed, networked, multi-tiered, single and multi-platform configurations and variants thereof.

A major theme to be reiterated throughout the use of the DoD TRM document itself is that:
While the model is not formally mandated in all acquisitions, consistent use of service and interface definitions contained in the DoD TRM document is essential if interoperability is to be achieved. In this manner, the war fighter can achieve a higher degree of interoperability across systems that can effectively fulfil mission requirements. Therefore, a key interoperability and open system requirement to be stressed in developments is to utilize the model's definitions first, before attempting to develop new ones. Use of model definitions and classes provides further assurance to other DoD stakeholders that a common foundation is being used across a broad range of DoD applications and the operational environment.

The DoD TRM is the foundation for both the JTA and DII COE. Service categories contained in the latter two programs are derived from the DoD TRM definitions Initiatives aimed at developing tailored or model variants thereof (e.g., functional model) should first draw from the structure and definitions contained in the DoD TRM in order to maintain the same consistency of service or interface definitions throughout DoD.

22.4 Principles

Within DoD and industry, a number of standards-based architecture methodologies can be found that address interoperability and open system issues. While the number of methodology steps may vary across them, the overall set of work tasks and activities contained therein address more or less the same issues. In general, the first step or activity of an architectural methodology focuses on identifying policy and requirements to justify the course of action to be taken. The next two steps provide insight into the technical aspects of using a reference model to characterize the existing architecture to the extent it exists, and to identify the "To-Be" architecture. While the second step of the methodology generally focuses on capturing the as-is architecture, subsequent steps focus on the development of the to-be architecture. It is in the latter steps that the technical reference model, specifically the DoD TRM, plays a significant role in addressing interoperability, open systems, and related technology issues. The architecture process is part of the overall development or acquisition process to ensure that interoperability is supported.

22.5 *Structure*

Phase 1:
- o Identify major objectives;
- o Identify relevant DoD policy, directives, instructions, etc.;
- o Identify key DoD requirements drivers from MNS, CRDs, ORDs, JROC, etc.;
- o Identify relevant program documentation, e.g., specifications, ICDs, system descriptions;
- o Assess and evaluate objectives against requirements;
- o Develop Architecture Statement-of Work and Memorandum of Understanding that identifies degree of commitment to interoperability issue.

Phase 2:
- o Identify enterprise issues (new or existing system);
- o Identify reference model used (existing system);

o Identify existing services and interfaces (existing system);
o Identify services and interfaces (new system);
o Perform mappings (new or existing system);
o Develop Baseline Characterization (new or existing system).

Phase 3:
o Identify complete set of functions, services and interfaces (new or additional ones);
o Develop tailored view (if needed);
o Perform comparative and trade-off analyses;
o Document Target Architecture or architecture issue.

22.5.1 Beyond Phase 2 and 3

Subsequent phases in various methodologies focus on the prioritisation of the added or new functionality to be implemented as a function of cost, schedule, and other benefits. Subsequent methodology steps include migration planning that allows the sequencing of work tasks or incremental development. Actual architecture development subsequently begins and is followed by maintenance tasks that provide for the continuous monitoring of such items as changes in technology, doctrine, or environment changes.

22.6 Guidance

The model is to be used when addressing the following interoperability issues:

o When consistent and extensive service and interface terminology is required to address or describe an interoperability issue;
o When functional analysis is to be performed and similar functions must be compared, matched, assessed or

evaluated with other functions either within the same system or between disparate systems;

o When mappings of services and interfaces are to be performed for the purpose of com-paring functionality, products or standards;

o When addressing migration issues that require knowledge of existing functionality, services and interfaces;

o In developing standards profiles that must be categorized against a set of services and interfaces.

o In developing different architecture views (e.g., technical, operational, system);

o In performing standards assessments to determine the degree of similarity, difference, non-applicability, completeness, orthogonality, or conflict within a standard or across standards;

o In assessing products for incorporation into a system or for replacement of system components;

o In assessing new technologies relative to the services or interfaces provided, and those that are impacted by the new or replacement technology;

o When tailored model views (domain specific models) are required to support an enterprise or weapon system functional area;

o When a framework is needed to support diverse platform configurations (e.g., client-server, networked, single and multi-processor configurations) and a representation of the services provided and interfaces contained within them must be developed.

The model can be used to address a range of technical architecture developments, interoperability, and open system issues. Further insight into architectural configurations can be found in the C4ISR Architecture Framework (C4ISR AF) document. In developing a technical architecture, the basic approach to using the model is to initially utilize the definitions and relationships established in the DoD TRM document rather than "invent" or develop new ones. When new services or interfaces are required, these should be forwarded to the TRMWG for consideration and incorporation into the next version of the DoD TRM document.

22.7 Compliance

DoD Technical Reference Model, Version 1.0.

The DoD Technical Reference Model (DOD TRM) Version 1.0 Promulgation Letter and document represents DoD's response to the need for a technical reference model. The Letter recognises the need for a TRM and the void created by the rescinding of the TAFIM. Prior to rescinding of the TAFIM, TAFIM Volume 2, Technical Reference Model provided a reference model to be used by DoD.

Compliance in terms of CCA is not part of DoD's TRM.

23 Technical Architecture Framework for Information Management (TAFIM)©

23.1 History

The latest version of US DoD TAFIM, Version 3.0, was published in 1996. Contractors and US DoD organisations have been applying this set of guidelines to current and future information systems. The US Defence Information Infrastructure Common Operating Environment is an implementation of TAFIM. It may take several years, after multiple new TAFIM-compliant systems are in the field, to determine the effectiveness of the reference model with respect to achieving a common, flexible, and interoperable DoD infrastructure.

The TAFIM has been rescinded via Architecture Coordinating Council (ACC) Memo, dated 7 January, 2000, Subject: DoD Policy Change -- Cancellation of the Technical Architecture Framework for Information Management (TAFIM).

The ACC's Technical Architecture Steering Group (TASG) finalised the re-evaluation of the TAFIM in 2000. The TASG concluded that the TAFIM as a collective entry is inconsistent with the new DoD architecture direction. Further, the TASG recognised that TAFIM legacy elements, such as a Technical Reference Model (TRM), need to be continued since it is the source for the DoD Joint Technical Architecture (JTA) and Defence Information Infrastructure, Common Operating Environment as well as DoD's compliance with the Clinger Cohen Act.

© *US Department of Defence; Source: Technical Architecture Framework for Information Management (TAFIM), Version 3.0; http://www-library.itsi.disa.mil/tafim/*

The mandate for the use of TAFIM as collective entity is rescinded and references to TAFIM will be removed from all DoD documentation.

24 Computer Integrated Manufacturing Open System Architecture (CIMOSA)©

24.1 History

CIMOSA is a well-known CIM Open System Architecture developed by the AMICE Consortium, and the most important CIM initiative within the former European ESPRIT program. The term AMICE is a reversed acronym for 'European CIM Architecture'. CIMOSA is an European Standard.

24.2 Purpose

The aim of this project was to elaborate an open system architecture for CIM and to define a set of concepts and rules to facilitate the building of future CIM systems. An important aspect of the project is its direct involvement in standardization activities. The two main results of the project are the Modelling Framework, which is well known and the Integrating Infrastructure.

24.3 Scope

The Modelling Framework supports all phases of the CIM system life cycle from requirements definition, through design specification, implementation description and execution of the daily enterprise operation. The Integrating Infrastructure provides specific information technology services for the execution of the Particular Implementation Model, but what is

---

© *CIMOSA Association; http://www.cimosa.de/index.html*

more important, it provides for vendor independence and portability.

The primary objective of CIMOSA is to provide a framework for analysing the evolving requirements of an enterprise and translating these into a system, which enables and integrates the functions, which match the requirements. *See European normative work:* **Framework for Enterprise Modelling** *CEN/TC 310 ENV 40003.*

The CIMOSA Reference Architecture contains a limited set of architectural constructs to completely describe the requirement of and the solutions for a particular enterprise. *See European normative work:* **Constructs for Enterprise Modelling** *CEN/TC 310 ENV 12204.*

Computer Integrated Manufacturing should provide to the industry opportunities to streamline production flows, to reduce lead times and to increase overall quality while adapting the enterprise fully to the market needs. Adaptability and Flexibility in a turbulent environment is a key issue.

CIMOSA provides a widely accepted CIM concept with an adequate set of architectural constructs to structure CIM Systems.

This concept is based on an unambiguous terminology in order to serve as a common technical base for CIM system users, CIM system developers and CIM components suppliers.

CIMOSA provides us with an architectural framework to help thinking the integrated enterprise through its various views.

24.4 Principles

The generalised **concept of Isolation** gives solutions to most of the questions raised before.

In particular, the concept of *Object View*, which isolates any Application from the Enterprise Object it operates upon, enables building Applications accessing the right Object View through a neutral service (*System Wide Information Services*) without knowing the structure of the Enterprise Object this Object View refers to.

The CIMOSA architectural principles are based on the generalised concept of isolation:

o **Isolation between the User representation and the System representation** which restricts the impact of changes and provides ability to modify the enterprise behaviour in order to cope with market changes (organisational flexibility);

o **Isolation between Control and Functions** making possible to revise the enterprise behaviour, in order to meet changing circumstance, without altering the installed functionality;

o **Isolation between Functions and Information** to facilitate integration, application portability, inter-operability and maintainability.

24.5 Structure

The CIMOSA modelling framework (*CIMOSA cube*) is based upon:

24.5.1 A dimension of Generality

(Three architectural levels)

Generic level	Catalogue of basic building blocks
Partial level	Library of partial models applicable to particular purposes

Particular level	Model of a particular enterprise built from building blocks and partial models

24.5.2   A dimension of Model

(Three modelling levels)

Requirements Modelling.	For gathering business requirements	*Business User*
Design Modelling	For specifying optimised and system-oriented representation of the business requirements	System Designer
Implementation Modelling	For describing a complete CIM system and all its implemented components	System Developer

24.5.3   A dimension of View

(To describe the Model according to its four integrated aspects)

Function View.	For describing the expected behaviour and functionality of the enterprise
Information View	For describing the integrated information objects of the enterprise
Resource View	For describing the resource objects of the enterprise
Organisation View	For describing the organisation of the enterprise

24.6   *Guidance*

The concept of "Enterprise Integration" is a response to the current situation where enterprises are still a juxtaposition of "islands of automation". It embraces all technologies required to make working together   actors participating to *enterprise engineering* and *enterprise operation*.

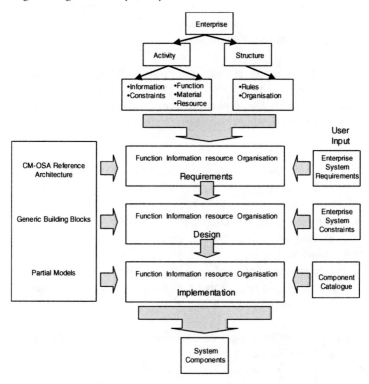

CM-OSA Modelling Levels and derivation Process for
CM-OSA Particular Architecture

From an **enterprise engineering viewpoint**, the key factor is to provide actors (namely, the Business User, the Designer and component Suppliers -machines and software-) with a common culture (and language) to communicate and make sure that:

o Requirements expressed by the Business User are well translated into system specifications, (I prefer the term "sub-system" to show that any development is just a part of the **Integrated Enterprise System**);

o System specifications are correctly translated into system components able to be added and removed to the Enterprise System without negative impact to the installed functionality, (Keep in mind that the **enterprise is in permanent change!**).

From an **enterprise operation viewpoint**, the key factor is to provide actors (namely, the Machines, Human Beings and Applications) with the means to communicate between them and Information they share and exchange. That requires solution to:

o *Business Integration*, i.e.; how Applications, Machines and Human Beings can be support together a particular Business Process;

o *Application Inter-Operability*, i.e. how Applications can access and understand common Enterprise Objects (need of "universal" Data Models);

o *Information Integration*, i.e.; how the different views all Applications need can be put together to form a global Enterprise Object.

In addition, how making possible the permanent evolving of Enterprise Objects resulting from the evolution of the business without impacting installed functionality?

24.7 Compliance

There is no compliancy with the CCA, however the CIMOSA modelling framework has been adopted by CEN/CENELEC as the European pre-standard for CIM enterprise modelling, where it is known as ENV 40003.

Related standards:

- **ISA 95.00.01-2000:** 'Enterprise-Control System Integration, ISO/IEC JWG15, 2001
- **EN 19439:** Framework for Enterprise Modelling, CEN TC 310/WG1 - ISO TC 184/SC5/WG1, 2001
- **ENV 13550:** Advanced Manufacturing Technology - Systems Architecture - Enterprise Model Execution and Integration Services, CEN/TC310, 1999
- **ENV 40003:** Computer Integrated Manufacturing - Systems Architecture - Framework for Enterprise Modelling, CEN/CENELEC, 1991

25 Purdue Enterprise Reference Architecture (PERA) ©

25.1 *History*

During the period 1989-1992, research at Purdue Laboratory for Applied Industrial Control *[PLAIC]* was devoted almost exclusively to servicing the Industry-Purdue University Consortium on Computer Integrated Manufacturing (CIM). The group of ten companies developed, with major input from PLAIC, an *Implementation Procedures Manual for Computer Integrated Manufacturing.*

The manual outlines in a complete, step-by-step manner the preparation of detailed Master Plans for implementing CIM in any factory of any company, regardless of industry. Formal work on the Manual was completed with its publication on June 8, 1992.

Also completed at the same time was the related publication entitled, *The Purdue Enterprise Reference Architecture,* described just below.

The successful pursuit of the *Implementation Procedures Manual* hinged upon the parallel development of a better method of describing the modelling of an enterprise system and particularly a method for describing the place of the human in the development and operation of such systems.

This was accomplished with the completion of *The Purdue Enterprise Reference Architecture (PERA).* PERA has shown itself

---

© *Perdue Laboratory for Applied Industrial Control; Source: http://pera.net/*

to be the easiest understood and most capable reference architecture in the public domain today. It has demonstrated its ability to model any enterprise, regardless of industry or field of endeavour. It is also the only one known to us, which explicitly treats all aspects of the involvement of the human in an enterprise system.

With the completion of *the* Implementation Procedures Manual, the Industrial Consortium was disbanded but related work continued in PLAIC with a new group entitled *"The Industry-Purdue CIM Architecture Users Group."*

The Users Group continued the work initiated by the Consortium and in addition worked to exploit the capabilities shown by the architecture. The architecture was enthusiastically accepted by the members of the Consortium, the Users Group, and all others who reviewed it.

Work at the Purdue Laboratory for Applied Industrial Control during the 1991-1992 period concentrated on the further development and promulgation of the Purdue Enterprise Reference Architecture and Methodology for planning and implementing enterprise integration (CIM) programs as developed from the Industry-Purdue Consortium for CIM. This also involved major involvement in directing the work of the International Task Force on Architectures for Enterprise Integration of which Professor Williams was Chairman.

25.2 Purpose

If you do not know where you are going, you probably will not get there.

Although this seems self-evident, most corporations today do not have a Master Plan for integrating new computing and communications technology. Yet, there are many examples of companies like Federal Express and Gateway Computers, who have demonstrated that improving the use of information, can provide a decisive competitive advantage.

This is equally true of any major new facility or expansion. Typically, Project Managers are focused on building the physical facility, and the business managers who will be responsible for making the new facility work, are not yet assigned. The failure to plan for information systems and human and organisational aspects during the facility-engineering phase, commonly results in a facility, which is physically, complete, but which takes months to start up and reach its profit potential.

25.3 Scope

The PERA Master Planning Methodology provides a methodical approach to planning which can be used at any phase in the life cycle of an enterprise.

The PERA Framework provides a framework for planning each phase of the enterprise. As such, it encompasses all other planning, design, and analysis tools.

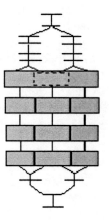

Both of the above PERA diagrams emphasize the importance of considering Human and Organisational aspects, as well as Control and Information Systems, at every phase of the enterprise.

25.4 Principles

There are only 3 major components of any enterprise:
  o   Physical Plant
  o   People
  o   Information Systems

PERA provides a life cycle model, which demonstrates how to integrate Enterprise Systems, Physical Plant Engineering and Organisational Development from enterprise concept to dissolution.
Since the physical plant is the most obvious component of an enterprise, many people think of a corporation only in terms of its physical assets.

However, although they do not show up on a balance sheet, people are often more important than physical assets to a company's long-term competitive position.

Information, communications and control systems comprise the third component. Without an effective "nervous system" provided by a modern enterprise information and communication system, the enterprise will be sluggish and soon overtaken by competitors that are more agile.

PERA clearly defines the roles and relationships among physical plant, people, and information systems.

25.5 Structure

The PERA Model breaks the enterprise life cycle into "phases" as follows. While this is not the only possible "phase breakdown", it is one, which has been proven in a large number of projects in many industries. It also breaks the investment approval process into a number of steps, which works well for projects larger than a few million dollars. Smaller projects may combine phases to reduce overhead costs, but the deliverables between phases generally remain the same.

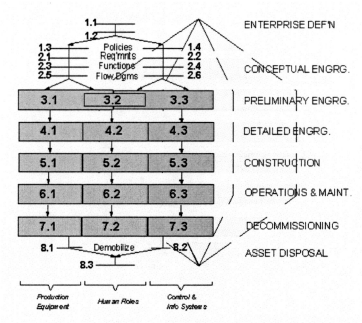

At the end of each phase, a well-defined set of "deliverables" should be produced. These typically include drawings, calculations, computer models, cost estimates, economic analyses, etc.

Since the development of the next phase is based on these deliverables, approval to proceed to the next project phase should be contingent upon acceptance and approval of ALL deliverables from the previous phase. Failure to do so virtually guarantees recycle and lost time and cost in the subsequent phase.

Example Enterprise Activities

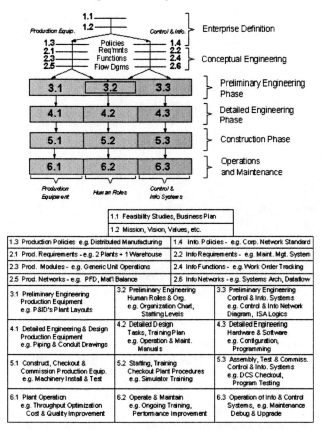

1.1 Feasibility Studies, Business Plan		
1.2 Mission, Vision, Values, etc.		
1.3 Production Policies e.g. Distributed Manufacturing	1.4 Info. Policies - e.g. Corp. Network Standard	
2.1 Prod. Requirements - e.g. 2 Plants + 1 Warehouse	2.2 Info Requirements - e.g. Maint. Mgt. System	
2.3 Prod. Modules - e.g. Generic Unit Operations	2.4 Info Functions - e.g. Work Order Tracking	
2.5 Prod. Networks - e.g. PFD, Mat'l Balance	2.6 Info Networks - e.g. Systems Arch, Dataflow	
3.1 Preliminary Engineering Production Equipment e.g. P&ID's Plant Layouts	3.2 Preliminary Engineering Human Roles & Org. e.g. Organization Chart, Staffing Levels	3.3 Preliminary Engineering Control & Info. Systems e.g. Control & Info Network Diagram, ISA Logics
4.1 Detailed Engineering & Design Production Equipment e.g. Piping & Conduit Drawings	4.2 Detailed Design Tasks, Training Plan e.g. Operation & Maint. Manuals	4.3 Detailed Engineering Hardware & Software e.g. Configuration, Programming
5.1 Construct, Checkout & Commission Production Equip. e.g. Machinery Install & Test	5.2 Staffing, Training Checkout Plant Procedures e.g. Simulator Training	5.3 Assembly, Test & Commiss. Control & Info. Systems e.g. DCS Checkout, Program Testing
6.1 Plant Operation e.g. Throughput Optimization Cost & Quality Improvement	6.2 Operate & Maintain e.g. Ongoing Training, Performance Improvement	6.3 Operation of Info & Control Systems, e.g. Maintenance Debug & Upgrade

Similarly, subsequent changes to even small details in these "previous phase" deliverables will have a domino effect on current phase deliverables. As the project proceeds, it becomes more and more difficult to "improve" the design, since the cost and delay caused by changes becomes progressively greater.

As the PERA model indicates there are also interfaces within the phase. At the highest level, these are between the three main enterprise components (Production Facilities, People, and

Control and Information Systems). However, each of these is typically further sub-divided on large projects. The numbers of sub-divisions increase as the project progresses (and staffing increases). This is necessary to bring additional resources and skills to bear, however each additional interface presents communication barriers, which are perhaps the most difficult aspect of large project execution.

Most experienced project managers have an intuitive appreciation of the nature of this problem; however a better understanding of the reasons behind it can help minimize its effects.

25.6 Guidance

The design and implementation of an enterprise must be effectively integrated with Enterprise Systems planning, human, and Organisational development.

PERA divides the enterprise life cycle into "phases" as follows.

At the end of each development phase, a set of "Deliverables" are produced such as those indicated below. Note these deliverables are typical of a process industry facility such as a refinery, power plant, pipeline, etc.; however similar deliverables would be produced for a service industry, or discrete manufacturing enterprise.

It is vitally important that the interfaces between groups who are designing the enterprise are clearly understood and coordinated.

For example, during the Preliminary Engineering Phase, when the manufacturing process is being defined, the control and information systems, and the human roles are also being developed in parallel.

PERA defines the concept of maximum and minimum lines of automation for both the manufacturing facility and the control and information system. The PERA model makes it clear that as levels of automation of physical plant or control and information systems change, the human role is immediately changed.

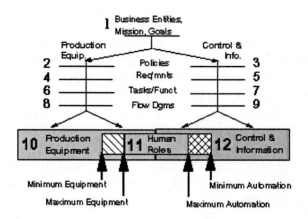

25.7 *Compliance*

PERA is not compliant with the CCA. PERA is currently proposed as the basis for an international IFAC/IFIP standard. The Purdue Architecture and the Purdue Methodology (PERA) for CIM has been accepted as a major component of the overall internationally proposed architecture and methodology.

26 Standards and Architectures for eGovernment Applications (SAGA)©

26.1 History

With the Standards and Architectures for eGovernment Applications (SAGA), the German Federal Government is making an important contribution towards modern and service-orientated administration. In September 2000, Chancellor Gerhard Schröder launched the BundOnline 2005 e-government initiative and obliged the Federal administration to provide its more than 350 Internet-enabled services online by the year 2005. Federal administrations, agencies and authorities have started implementing this initiative.

Since the end of 2002, more than 160 administration services have now become available online.

Coordinated by the German Federal Ministry of the Interior (BMI), an implementation plan was drafted and basic components defined. These basic components and applications that were developed according to the "one-for-all" principle, as well as new e-government applications to be created during the years to come are to smoothly interact with each other. A uniform "look and feel" system is to be made available to users.

Following the development of the implementation plan, the Federal Ministry of the Interior set up a project group responsible for developing concrete technical procedures for this implementation plan.

© *German Federal Ministry of the Interior in co-operation with the German Federal Office for Information Security; Source: http://kbst.bund.de/saga*

The first step involved taking stock of existing standards which was carried out by a group that included eight experts from industry and another six experts from Federal-government, Federal-state and communal administrations.

This was the basis for the development of the Standards and Architectures for eGovernment Applications (SAGA).

The resolution by the Federal Government on security in electronic legal and business matters with the Federal administration of 16 January 2002 was taken into consideration, as was the "Verordnung zur Schaffung barrierefreier Informationstechnik nach dem Behindertengleichstellungsgesetz (Barrierefreie Informationstechnik Verordnung BITV)" (Ordinance on the creation of barrier-free information technology pursuant to the law on equal opportunities for the disabled (barrier-free information technology ordinance (BITV)).

26.2 Purpose

SAGA pursues the following aims:

- o To ensure ongoing flows of information between citizens, the Federal Government and its partners (interoperability);
- o To establish comparable procedures for the provision of services and for the definition of data models (re-usability). German Federal-state governments and communal administrations have the opportunity to make use of the development results of the BundOnline 2005 initiative;
- o To provide specifications in the form of publicly accessible documentation (openness);
- o To consider developments on the market and in the field of standardization (cost and risk reduction);

o To ensure the applicability of solutions against the background of changing requirements in terms of volume and transaction frequencies (scalability).

26.3 Scope

SAGA is a standardization project with an integrated approach that explains all the aspects necessary to achieve the aforementioned objectives. Standards or architectures not mentioned:

o Are not specific for e-government or e-commerce applications;
o Refer to a detail level other than that of the standards dealt with here in SAGA;
o Are included in or referenced by the aforementioned standards;
o Are too new or too controversial in order to be likely to become a standard in the new future;
o Are not desired because they conflict with standards or architectures already introduced or because they restrict interoperability.

26.4 Principles

Modern e-government calls for interoperable information and communication systems that (ideally) interact smoothly. Simple and clear-cut standards and specifications help to achieve interoperability of information and communication systems. SAGA identifies the necessary standards, formats and specifications; it sets forth conformity rules and updates these in line with technological progress.

E-government applications are developed in accordance with the following basic principles:

o E-government applications primarily use the browser as their front-end, unless the services to be implemented cannot be reasonably handled via a browser;

o They forego active contents, to that users are not forced to reduce the browser's security settings, which could result in damage by invisible Internet pages, or they at least use only signed and quality-secured applications;

o E-government applications do not store any program parts or data on the users' computers beyond the users' control.

26.5 Structure

The document defines three target groups for the Federal administration's services (refer to the selection shown in the next figure):

o Government to citizens: services which the Federal Government offers its citizens directly;

o Government to business: services, which the Federal Government offers to companies;

o Government to government: Federal Government services for public agencies.

More than 350 services of the different Federal administrations were identified. An analysis of the services along the value chain enabled the identification of eight service types (refer to www.bundonline2005.de). 73 percent of the services used today already belong to the three following types:

o Gathering, processing and providing information;

o Processing applications and requests sent to public agencies;

o Processing subsidy and assistance applications.

G2C Government to Citizen	G2B Government to Business	G2G Government to Goverment
• BA: Job exchange • BA: Payments • BfA: Calculation and payment of pensions • BMA: Provision of information • BA: Advice • BfA: Advice • DWD: Weather forecasts and meteorological advice • BfA: Collection of pension scheme contributions • BEV: Cost refunds within the scope of health and disability schemes for civil servants • BZgA: Provision of specialist and technical information (on health education) • BpB: Provision of information and order handling • BAFA: Promotion of renewable energies	• BA: Job exchange • KBA: Management of central transport and motor vehicle register • BeschA: Procurement • BBR: Procurement for construction and civil engineering projects • BZV: Customs clearance, exports and imports • StBA: Central statistics • BMBF: Project-related subsidies • BMWi: Subsidy programmes • BaKred: Information on issues relevant for bank regulatory authorities • BIF: Assignment of VAT numbers • EBA: Awarding procedures pursuant to VOL/A, VOB/A, VOF • RegTP: Assignment of telephone numbers • BA: Provision of information	• BeschA: Procurement • BfF: Central cashier's office of the Federal Government • BBR: Procurement for construction and civil engineering projects • BMF: Management of Federal Government properties • BAkÖV: Further training and education • StBA: Central statistics • BZR: Federal Central Register of Criminal Offences • BZR: Information from the central commercial register

26.5.1 SAGA Reference Model

The model of the architecture kit in SAGA serves the following purposes:

o   In order to facilitate communications, a common understanding of up-to-date IT architectures and technologies as well as e-government structures is to be achieved;

o   IT technologies available for e-government applications are to be identified, compared, evaluated with regard to their relevance, and given a uniform and consistent structure using this model;

o   The aim is to provide standards that can be used when it comes to the implementation of e-government projects.

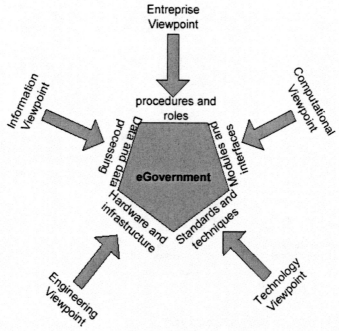

SAGA Reference Model for Open Distributed Processing

A view of an application under different viewpoints is helpful in order to describe complex, distributed   e-government applications. Breaking down into viewpoints reduces the complexity of the individual viewpoints.

26.5.1.1 RM-ODP

The Reference Model for Open Distributed Processing (RM ODP) proposes five viewpoints for a system, which are adopted for SAGA.

1. The Enterprise Viewpoint specifies purposes, scope, processes and policies for an application;

2. The Information Viewpoint describes the characteristics and semantics of the data processed, as well as the detailed processes for data processing;
3. The Computational Viewpoint represents the breaking down of an application into functional modules and their interaction interfaces;
4. The Engineering Viewpoint represents the distribution of the individual elements of the system to physical resources and their connections;
5. The Technology Viewpoint describes the technologies used to implement the system;

The five viewpoints can be used both to describe existing systems and to model new systems and applications.

26.6 Guidance

Trials with standards and architectures for e-government have been underway for some years now in Germany and in other countries. Experience from these trials and international exchange contribute towards facilitating the definition and implementation of SAGA. Some generally accepted factors for the success of e-government are as follows:

Legislative framework

The legislative framework must enable a user-friendly and efficient supply of services on the Internet.
Customer data (i.e. data on citizens, companies or public agencies), for example, must be electronically stored to a certain extent in order to offer users a user-friendly interface and to more than just information services.

Process definitions and Meta data

A uniform and standardized process and data definition is a precondition for uniform and standardized hardware, applications and interfaces.

Training

The use and updating of standards means an ongoing exchange of information and training process. Activities of this kind are organised via the Federal Ministry of the Interior and/or the BundOnline 2005 project group.

26.7 Compliancy

There is no CCA compliancy.

Enterprise Architecture Tools

27 Enterprise Architecture Tools

27.1 Introduction

Enterprise Architectures are an emerging approach for capturing complex knowledge about organizations and technology. Enterprise Architectural approaches range from broad, enterprise focused approaches, through to approaches aimed at specific domains.

The focus of enterprise architecture efforts is now shifting to become more holistic, thereby necessitating the use of comprehensive modelling tools to analyze and optimize the portfolio of business strategies, organizational structures, business processes / tasks and activities, information flows, applications, and technology infrastructure.

Important to adoption of an enterprise architectural approach is the availability of tools to support the development, storage, presentation and enhancement of enterprise architecture representations. As with enterprise architecture methodologies, enterprise architecture tools to support the architectural development process are still emerging.

High value is derived from consolidating this portfolio of business artefacts into a single repository in a standardized manner to support enterprise analysis and optimization. *[Report, Australian Defense Force, 2001]*

27.2 Enterprise Architecture Tools Review

To consistently review enterprise architecture tools a review approach is defined. The review approach consists of two dimensions: the basic functionality of the tool, and the utility of the tool to different professionals.

When reviewing an EA tool's basic functionality, the reviewer has to describe how well the tool performed the different functions needed for the enterprise architecture development activity. The tools basic functionality was examined in the following areas: Methodologies and Models; Model Development Interface; Tool Automation; Extendibility and Customization; Analysis and Manipulation; Repository.

The second dimension, the tool's utility to different professionals, captures the fitness for purpose of the tool, and describes how useful the tool would be to particular professionals. The types of professionals considered were: Enterprise Architects; Strategic Planners; Enterprise Program Managers.

27.3 Functionality Dimension

This dimension of the EA Tools review approach attempts to capture how well the tool performs the core functions needed to support the enterprise architecture development activity. This dimension breaks the functionality of an enterprise architecture tool into eight key areas.

27.4 Methodologies and Models

The most important feature of an enterprise architecture tool the methodologies and modelling the approaches it supports. The approaches the tool supports dictate the types of enterprise architectures the tool is capable of supporting, and to an extent, the type of analysis and manipulation functions the tool is capable of performing. As well as reviewing the methodologies and modelling approaches, this functional area also reviews how well, or how completely, the tool implements the methodologies and modelling approaches it claims to support.

27.5 Model Development Interface

The model development interface is the most obvious part of an enterprise architecture development tool. It is the interface used to design, build, maintain and often manipulate, the models that make up the architecture. Generally, models are built and maintained graphically, by manipulating icons and the connections between them. The tool's model development interface may also use textual interfaces to allow additional information to be appended to the graphical models.

The overall quality of the model development interface is an important characteristic of any enterprise architecture development tool. The interface must support the modelling activity well, for example by automating some of the drawing functions, by automatically laying out models, or by providing pick lists of alternative values at the appropriate places during the modelling activity. The model development interface must also be intelligently structured, make good use of limited screen space, be logical and consistent to use and navigate. The tool should ideally follow the graphical user interface conventions and guidelines that apply to its host operating system.

27.6 Tool Automation

Developing and populating enterprise architecture models is often the most time consuming part of the enterprise architecture development activity. By providing support for automating parts of the enterprise architecture development processes, a tool can help speed up the overall development activity.

A tool may also provide the ability to automatically generate enterprise architecture models based on data held within the tool's repository, or have the ability to generate enterprise architecture models as a result of data manipulation functions.

27.7 Extendibility and Customization

This functional group captures how well an enterprise architecture tool can be modified to meet the unique enterprise architectural requirements of a unique organization. Enterprise Architecture tools may support customization by allowing users to add new modelling approaches or to modify the modelling approaches already supported by the tool. A tool may also support modification by providing a programming interface, allowing the functions of the tool to be modified, or allowing the tool to be integrated with other software products. Most enterprise architecture tools that support high levels of customization allow the underlying meta-models of the tool to be modified, and new meta-models added. The ability to modify the tool via a programming interface allows the functionality and behaviour of the tool to be customized to meet the unique requirements of the organization.

27.8 Analysis and Manipulation

As well as supporting the development of enterprise architecture models, an enterprise architecture tool may also provide support for analysis and manipulation of the developed models. The type of analysis and manipulation support provided by the tool is often tied to the particular modelling approaches supported by the tool. For example, Flow Analysis is often tied to process/workflow modelling.

Analysis support provided by a tool may simply examine how correct or complete the model is, relative to a particular modelling approach used. More sophisticated analysis support may allow the model to be interrogated in some way, or be subjected to particular analysis methods. Analysis support may include the ability to compare different versions of models, allowing current and to-be enterprise architectures to be compared. Manipulation functions capture a tool's ability to change the way the models are represented and viewed. This may include the ability to view models from particular perspectives, for example showing only particular classes of entities, or the ability to amalgamate separate models into a single model.

27.9 Repository

Most of the tools on the market make use of some kind of data repository to hold the developed models. The functions provided by the tool's repository have a significant impact on the overall functionality, scalability and extendibility of an enterprise architecture tool.

Some tools make use of commercial relational database management systems, or commercial Object Orientated or Object/Relational database systems, while others use proprietary repository systems.

A tool's repository often dictates the way users can collaborate. A repository may provide support for collaboration by supporting multiple, concurrent, users on the one repository, or by providing the ability to combine models developed by different modellers into one model.

The repository may also provide many different data management functions, including the ability to support model versioning, the ability to roll back to previous versions, the ability to lock parts of the model against change, and the ability to control access to part or the entire model.

27.10 *Overview of popular EA Tools*

Enterprise Architecture Tools Overview			Updated 07-2004
Company	**Products**	**Framework Support**	**Development Facilities**
ASG Software Solutions	Rochade		Broad scope of facilities
Méga International	Méga	Zachman	
Troux	Troux		
Agilense	EA Webmodeler	Agilense, Synthesis, Zachman, TOGAF, DoDAF, FEAF/TEAF, FEA	Fully programmable, interfaces with other tools
US Government	FEAMS	FEAF, TEAF, C4ISR	
Flashline	FlashPack	FEAF	
LogicLibrary	Logidex		Software development asset (SDA) mapping and discovery engine
Adaptive	Adaptive IT Portfolio Manager		
Alfabet	Strategic IT Management Solution Framework	SITM framework	
Casewise	Corporate Modeler Enterprise Edition	Casewise Framework, Zachman	Rational Rose, Erwin, PowerDesigner, OracleDesigner, Tibco, Telelogic Doors
Computas	Metis Product Familiy	Zachman, TOGAF, DoDAF, FEAF / TEAF	UML 2.0
IDS Scheer	ARIS Collaborative Suite	ARIS Framework	
Popkin Software	System Architect Family	Zachman, TOGAF 8, DoDAF	Business Process Modeling, IDEF, Gane and Sarson, Yourdon/DeMarco, Ward and Mellor, SSADM method, UML, XML
Proforma	Provision Modeling Suite	Zachman, C4ISR	Rummler-Brache, LOVEM, IDEF, UML, Visio, RUP, ERwin
Ptech	Enterprise Framework	Zachman, C4ISR	UML
Select Business Solutions	Select Enterprise	Zachman	MDA, UML, RUP, Yourdon, XP
Visible	Visible Advantage		IDEF1X and IDEF0

28 Examples of some EA Repository Tools & Suites

28.1 USA-Federal Enterprise Architecture Management System©

The Federal Enterprise Architecture Management System *[FEAMS]* tool is a U.S. government-owned, Web-based tool used to track and analyse an organisation's enterprise architecture. As an automated tool, FEAMS simplifies the management of a large amount of information and provides access to this information, relationships among information elements, and work products.

FEAMS is becoming a popular tool in the USA federal IT community with approximately 21 federal organisations in the process of reviewing or implementing it. FEAMS is not perfect, and several "early adopter" organisations have identified necessary modifications and desired enhancements. However, it does not make business sense to have separate federal organisations making enhancements to FEAMS at the same time. Doing so could result in: -- Spending money for multiple fixes to the same problem simultaneously, -- FEAMS --fracturing-- with multiple incompatible versions of FEAMS arising, and -- An uncoordinated approach that puts the government in a weak negotiating position when dealing with support contractors and will most likely lead to higher support costs.

Thus, a consortium of federal agencies is working to manage FEAMS an open source development project. Specifically, the U.S. Departments of Housing and Urban Development, Agriculture, and Labour, and the National Technology Alliance

---

© *U.S. government; Source: http://feapmo.gov/feams.asp*

arm of the National Imagery and Mapping Agency are in the process of taking FEAMS open source.

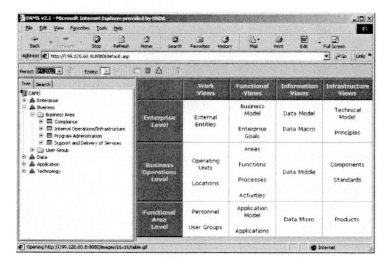

FEAMS-Tool

28.2 Popkin System Architect©

System Architect® is a comprehensive and powerful modelling solution designed to provide all of the tools necessary for development of successful enterprise systems. It is the only tool to integrate, in one multi-user product, industry-leading support for all major areas of modelling, including business process modelling, object-oriented and component modelling with UML, relational data modelling, and structured analysis and design. All functionality is harnessed within System Architect's extensible repository with native support for Microsoft VBA.

© *Popkin Software; System Architect is registered by Popkin Software; Source: http://www.popkin.com/*

Over the last few years, organisations have become more aware of the growing need to develop integrated models of their business in order to remain competitive and flexible to change.

To this end, interest in industry-accepted Enterprise Architecture Frameworks (for example, the **Zachman Framework** and **DoDAF** (C4ISR Framework)) has increased dramatically.

The System Architect: *Framework Manager*

To make navigating and viewing all of these models easier from a framework perspective, the new System Architect Framework Manager has been introduced. The System Architect Framework Manager enables users to view and access the models and artefacts they have developed in a System Architect encyclopaedia through a framework interface. Each cell of the framework can be opened to view a filtered browser list of all diagrams and definitions in the encyclopaedia that pertain to that cell of the framework. Users may use predefined, industry accepted, frameworks such as the Zachman Framework or the US Department of Defence Architecture Framework (DODAF -- more commonly known as the C4ISR framework) that are provided by Popkin, or build their own framework browser to support their own custom framework.

28.3 Metis – Computas©

Metis® is a powerful visual modelling tool that helps you by using complex enterprise knowledge to answer critical questions and solve business problems. Metis® allows you to capture and link information in multiple areas of an enterprise, from products to processes to systems. View your enterprise as a whole or focus in on the details. By analysing information and

---

©*Computas Norway; Metis is registered by Computas; Source: http://www.metis.no/*

relationships, you can determine the effect of changes and make informed decisions about your business.

Metis® is consistently ranked as one of the world's leading products in the field. Metis was recently certified as TOGAF 7-compliant, and supports UML, C4ISR and TEAF/FEAF.

The field of Enterprise Architecture is one in which the strengths of Metis are clearly seen. In order to optimise the use of Information Technology by complex, often global organisations, Enterprise Architects need a tool that not only can represent complexity, but also aid in analysis, and in producing output that is intelligible to many different user groups. The Metis ITM (EA)-template provides the necessary starting point for a successful Enterprise Architecture.

Computas and its partners offer a rich selection of Metis® templates, meta-models and starter models, minimizing the time and resources required to create high-value, customized business solutions for your modelling needs.

Metis® templates support Enterprise Architecture, Process Modelling, Business Strategy, IT Architecture, Project Management, Document Knowledge Management, and many other model types. Metis® is unique in letting you integrate all these models into holistic, enterprise-wide model structures, thus enabling true Visual Enterprise Integration™.

28.4 MEGA Integrated Modelling Environment©

The MEGA Integrated Modeling Environment is supported by MEGA's common repository architecture. This robust, scalable, object-oriented repository fully supports enterprise architects teams ensuring the fullest collaboration and information sharing.

Through enterprise blueprints, business analysts, IT architects and development teams operate in an aligned and highly productive environment. Dedicated MEGA products facilitate a comprehensive and streamlined approach to business process and enterprise architecture design and implementation.

MEGA products are complemented with extensive administration facilities with full support for document and intranet publishing, repository import, /export and generation capabilities. MEGA Supervisor provides the team management facilities required for business and IT to deliver complex projects and specialized publishing requirements. MEGA products offer full customization capabilities that allow MEGA deliverables to accommodate the requirements of your organization.

28.4.1 MEGA Process

MEGA Process provides powerful analysis and design capability for capturing, mapping and documenting business processes and organizational structures. MEGA Process provides decision support and impact analysis for multiple design scenarios. Simulation features and variant management capability enable dynamic scenarios for costs and resource analysis. With scenarios comparison, MEGA Process unlocks the road to process optimization.

With its powerful Repository and easy to use graphical tools, MEGA Process captures and manages your company's business process maps. Use of the Repository ensures consistency and traceability e.g. changes a name in one model and has it automatically propagated to all other models using the same object. MEGA Process automatically produces documentation and HTML websites for sharing within the project team and to a wider company audience. Such documentation can be used as a decision making tool for business managers.

28.4.2 MEGA Architecture

MEGA Architecture delivers Business and IT Managers the reference maps they need to align and fully integrate business and IT. CIOs, IT Directors and Enterprise Architects can validate IT investments and minimize development costs and deployment risks.

MEGA Architecture provides advanced modeling features to build application portfolios and deliver the application perspective of Enterprise Architecture maps. MEGA Architecture provides an information flow centric approach that exposes how IT systems support enterprise business processes and operations. Using City Planning techniques, IT managers can establish plans for developing new applications and revising old applications based on the enterprises objectives and goals. Taking into account the fast changing business requirements and technology offering, IT Professionals can deliver continuous application optimization and cost reduction.

28.4.3 MEGA Designer

Analysis & Design Tools and Methodologies are key factors in developing flexible IT systems that are in alignment with business objectives and requirements.

MEGA Designer is the modeling based solution of choice to produce architecture for the development of responsive, adaptive new applications and to control and manage enterprise data assets.

29 Acronyms & Glossary

ADM	Architecture Development Method	TOGAF Architecture Development Method [http://www.opengroup.org/architecture/]
AF	Architecture Framework	Typically a collection of guidance for developing and or documenting Architectures.
CADM	Core Architecture Data Model	A formal model defining the data organisation for a repository of C4ISR/DoDAF-compliant architecture products.
C4ISR	Command, Control, Communications, Computers, Intelligence, Surveillance, and Reconnaissance	
CIMOSA	Computer Integrated Manufacturing Open System Architecture	European standard for enterprise system integration in the manufacturing environment
CIO	Chief Information Officer	
Clinger-Cohen	The Clinger-Cohen Act of 1996	Also known as the Information Technology Management Reform Act, or ITMRA [http://wwwoirm.nih.gov/policy/itmra.html]
CMM	Capability Maturity Model	Capability Maturity Model® is registered in the U.S. Patent and Trademark Office by Carnegie Mellon University.
COTS	Commercial off the Shelf	

DARS	US DoD Architecture Repository System	A DoD repository for approved architecture information compliant with the DoDAF.
DoD	US Department of Defence	
DoDAF	US Department of Defence Architecture Framework	
EA	Enterprise Architecture	The collection of information, models, technologies, processes, and plans that underlies organisational functions.
E2A	Extended Enterprise Architecture	E2A® & Extended Enterprise Architecture® are Service Marks of the Institute For Enterprise Architecture Developments, the Netherlands.
E2AF	Extended Enterprise Architecture Framework	Service Marks of the Institute For Enterprise Architecture Developments, the Netherlands.
E2AMM	Extended Enterprise Architecture Maturity Model	Service Marks of the Institute For Enterprise Architecture Developments, the Netherlands.
EAESC	Enterprise Architecture Executive Steering Committee	
EAP	Enterprise Architecture Planning	
EAPMO	Enterprise Architecture Program Management Office	The USA Federal Enterprise Architecture Program Management Office (FEA-PMO)
FEA	Federal Enterprise Architecture (USA)	[http://www.feapmo.gov]
FEAF	Federal Enterprise	

	Architecture Framework (USA)	
GOTS	GOTS	Government off the Shelf
GPRA	Government Performance and Results Act	[http://www.whitehouse.gov/omb/mgmt-gpra/gplaw2m.html]
IAF	Integrated Architecture Framework	Capgemini's Integrated Architecture Framework
IEEE	Institute of Electrical and Electronics Engineers	[http://www.ieee.org]
ITMRA	Information Technology Management Reform Act (USA)	Also known as the Clinger-Cohen Act [http://wwwoirm.nih.gov/policy/itmra.html]
ISO	International Organisation for Standardization	[http://www.iso.ch]
JTA	Joint Technical Architecture (USA)	The JTA is a compendium of technical standards either approved or potentially approvable for use in DoD systems.
OMG	Object Management Group	
OMB	USA, Office of Management and Budget (US)	[http://www.whitehouse.gov/omb/]
PERA	Purdue Enterprise Reference Framework	Standard for Enterprise Architecture in the manufacturing environment
SIB	Standards Information Base	TOGAF, Standards Information Base;[http://www.opengroup.org/sib.htm]

TAFIM   Technical   Architecture for Information Systems (USA DoD)

TEAF   Treasury   Enterprise Architecture Framework (USA)

TOGAF   The   Open   Group Architecture Framework [http://www.opengroup.org/architecture/]

TISAF   Treasury   Information Systems   Architecture Framework (USA)

TRM   Technical   Reference The Open Group or DoD TRM Model

W3C   World   Wide   Web [http://www.w3c.org] Consortium

ZIFA   Zachman Institute for [http://www.zifa.com] Framework Advancement

30 References & Bibliography

1. 'Extended Enterprise Architecture Maturity Model'SM; E2AMM v2.0; Published IFEAD, 2004.
2. Antoine de Saint-Exupery; *http://www.thinkexist.com/English/Author/x/Author_1147_3.htm*
3. Enterprise Architecture Survey 2003, IFEAD; *http://www.enterprise-architecture.info*
4. Gartner Inc.; *http://www3.gartner.com*
5. The Open Group; *http://www.opengroup.org/*
6. 'A Standard for Business Architecture description' McDavid D.W., published in IBM Systems Journal 1999.
7. 'Solution Sets'; White Paper, Interoperability Clearing House, USA, 2002.
8. Book 'Architectuur, besturingssysteem voor adaptieve organisaties' Rijsenbrij, Schekkerman, Hendrick, Publisher Lemma, 2002.
9. C4ISR Architecture Framework; Version 2.0, DoD, US 1997, USA.
10. Clinger-Cohen Act / Information Technology Management Reform Act, CCA / ITMA; USA.
11. Graham, Ian 1995; *Migrating to Object Technology*. Wokingham, England: Addison-Wesley.
12. US DoD Architecture Framework; Version 1.0, DoDAF.
13. The Federal Enterprise Architecture Framework, Version 1.1., US CIO Council.
14. IEEE 1471-2000; Institute of Electrical and Electronics Engineers; ANSI/IEEE 1471-2000 & IEEE 1003.23-1998.
15. The Software Productivity Consortium NFP, Inc.; Architecture; *http://www.software.org/pub/architecture/*
16. Institute For Enterprise Architecture Developments, IFEAD; The Netherlands; *http://www.enterprise-architecture.info*
17. Joint Technical Architecture (JTA); version 4.0, (Defence Information Systems Agency), USA.

18. King, 1995: "Creating a strategic capabilities architecture." *Information Systems Management*, Vol. 12, No. 1, pp. 67-69, 1995, William R. King, Professor University of Pittsburgh, USA.

19. Nolan & Mulryan: Richard L. Nolan and Dennis W. Mulryan, "Undertaking an Architecture Program," Stage by Stage, Vol. 7, Number 2 (March-April, 1987).

20. Porter; Book, 'Competitive Strategy'; Porter, Michael E. 1980.

21. Saarinen, 1956; Eero Saarinen, President of the Cranbrook Academy of Art.

22. Saint-Exupery; 'The Little Prince', Antoine de Saint-Exupery, 1900 – 1944.

23. Spewak, Steven H. 1992; *Enterprise Architecture Planning*. New York: John Wiley & Sons.

24. Gansler, Jacques S., Arthur L. Money, and John L. Woodward, Jr., 2000; TAFIM.

25. US Dept. of the Treasury 2000; The Treasury Enterprise Architecture Framework, Version 1.0.

26. The Open Group; TOGAF, Version 8.0.

27. Villiers de, D. J. 2001; Using the Zachman Framework to Assess the Rational Unified Process, The Rational Edge 2001.

28. Australian Defense Force; A Review of Architecture Tools, DSTO-TR-1139, 2001

29. Zachman, J. A. and J. F. Sowa 1992: Extending and Formalizing the Framework for Information Systems Architecture, *IBM Systems Journal*. (31) 3: 590-616 (1992).

30. Zachman, J. A.; The Zachman Institute For Framework Advancements.

31 Related Links

o   C4ISR Architecture Framework;
    http://www.defenselink.mil/c3i/org/cio/i3/

o   Zachman Institute for Framework Advancement;
    http://www.zifa.com/

o   The Federal Enterprise Architecture Framework, and the
    CIO Council Web page for information on FEAF;
    http://www.feapmo.gov/fea.asp

o   Joint Technical Architecture, JTA Development
    Organisations, Documents, and Participation Information;
    http://www-jta.itsi.disa.mil/

o   The Treasury Enterprise Architecture Framework and the
    Treasury Department official Web version of TEAF;
    http://www.ustreas.gov/offices/management/cio/teaf/

o   Extended Enterprise Architecture (E2A) Framework, the
    Institute For Enterprise Architecture Developments;
    http://www.enterprise-architecture.info

o   Technical Architecture Framework for Information
    Management (TAFIM), Version 3.0; US Department of
    Defence; *http://www-library.itsi.disa.mil/tafim/*

o   Federal Enterprise Architecture Management System;
    http://feapmo.gov/feams.asp

o   TOGAF Version 8: Enterprise Edition, the Open Group's
    official Web version of TOGAF;
    http://www.opengroup.org/architecture/togaf

o   CIMOSA Association; *http://www.cimosa.de/index.html*

o "Creating a strategic capabilities architecture." William R. King, Professor University of Pittsburgh, USA; *http://www.katz.pitt.edu/fac_pages/King.htm*

o Eero Saarinen; *http://www.vitruvio.ch/arc/masters/saarinen.htm*

o Antoine de Saint-Exupery; *http://www.thinkexist.com/English/Author/x/Author_1147_3.htm*

o The Open Group; *http://www.opengroup.org/*

o The USA Office of Management & Budget; *http://www.whitehouse.gov/omb/*

32 About the Author

 Jaap Schekkerman (1953) received an engineer's degree in electronic engineering and information technology and a degree in clinical chemistry and business economics.

From 1973 till 1974, he was working as a scientist at the Free University Amsterdam. From 1974 till 1985, he was Chief Information Officer at the Red Cross Hospital Beverwijk, the Netherlands.

In 1982, Schekkerman was awarded with the American Ames Award for his international awarded article about the developments in medical information technology and the influence on human beings.

From 1985 till 1995, he was Manager of a Research & Development department and Manager of a Technology Consulting Group at RAET N.V.
The focus of his R&D activities was at Information Systems Architecture and multi-user/multi-tasking programming.

In 1995, Schekkerman joined Capgemini and became the Thought Leader in the areas of Business Technology Strategy & Enterprise Architecture.

In 2001, Schekkerman founded the Institute For Enterprise Architecture Developments to do research and knowledge exchange around Enterprise Architecture.
This institute is today one of the most important EA sources of information in the world.

Schekkerman is giving lectures on the topics of Information Management & Enterprise Architecture at several Universities and training institutes.

Schekkerman has published several methods, articles and books on topics related to Enterprise Architecture and he is a frequently invited speaker on national and international congresses and symposia.

For his most recent publications go to the website of the Institute For Enterprise Architecture developments:
http://www.enterprise-architecture.info

Member ships:
- o   Alliance member of the Federal Enterprise Architecture Certification Institute, USA.
- o   Member of the 'MANYWORLDS' knowledge network of Business Thought Leaders, USA.
- o   Member of the IEEE 1471 (Recommended Practice for Architectural Description) working group of the Institute of Electrical and Electronic Engineers (IEEE) USA.
- o   Member of the World Wide Institute of Software Architects (WWISA) USA.
- o   Member of the Netherlands Society of Information Architects (GIA) NL.

ISBN 141201607-X

9 781412 016070